Disaster Recovery and Business Continuity

A quick guide for organisations and business managers

Third edition

Disaster Recovery and Business Continuity

A quick guide for organisations and business managers

Third edition

THEJENDRA B.S

IT Governance Publishing

IT Governance Publishing
IT Governance Limited
Unit 3, Clive Court
Bartholomew's Walk
Cambridgeshire Business Park
Ely, Cambridgeshire
CB7 4EA
United Kingdom

www.itgovernance.co.uk

First published in the United Kingdom in 2007 by IT Governance Publishing: 978-1-905356-14-0.

Second edition published in 2008: 978-1-905356-37-9.

Third edition published in 2014
ISBN: 978-1-84928-538-4

ABOUT THE AUTHOR

Thejendra B.S is an Information Technology (IT) manager for a software development firm in Bangalore, India. He has also worked in other countries, such as, Saudi Arabia, Dubai, Bahrain, Qatar, Singapore, and Australia.

His introduction to IT began over 20 years ago, when after gaining a degree in electronics he took on the role of field manager. Since then he has developed a wealth of experience and knowledge of IT, and is familiar with a wide range of roles including IT support, help desk, asset management and IT security.

Thejendra is experienced in the areas of disaster recovery (DR) and business continuity (BC). He has dealt with many organisations – of all sizes and nature of business – around the world and has implemented numerous small to large IT projects worth millions of pounds.

Visit his website *www.thejendra.com* for details on his other books and articles. He can be contacted on *thejendra@yahoo.com* or *thejendrabs@gmail.com*.

FOREWORD

The increasing dependence of organisations on IT systems and the growing range of threats they face, from an act of nature to a terrorist attack, means that organisations that are unprepared for the worst will not usually survive the unexpected. Therefore, over the last ten years disaster recovery and business continuity have become critical business issues.

Business continuity is one of the most important areas of operational risk. This was recognised by the regulatory authorities in the Basel Accord, legislation from the UK's Companies Act 2006 and the US Sarbanes-Oxley Act, which all require an organisation's directors to take appropriate action to identify and deal with operational risk. A significant development for companies that wish to identify and apply best management practice in mitigating this risk was the emergence of the British Standard BS25999, which was the world's first formal Standard for Business Continuity Management (BCM). It contained both the code of practice and specification for a management system against which an organisation can achieve third party accredited certification. BS25999 was replaced by ISO/IEC 22301 in 2012, which enables organisations to demonstrate to their customers and partners their planned business resilience, and those that have such a certificate will inevitably gain a competitive advantage over those that don't.

In the US, ISO/IEC 22301 feeds into the voluntary private sector preparedness (PS-Prep) accreditation and certification scheme, which is a nationally recognised programme to develop excellence in disaster recovery and business continuity planning.

For smaller organisations, this book is a welcome guide to all the key aspects of disaster recovery and business continuity.

Alan Calder

Founder and Executive Chairman
IT Governance Ltd.

PREFACE

DR and BC are often considered to be a costly, complex and over complicated task that can only be handled by specialists. Executives and managers of small or medium-sized organisations and IT departments often live with the misconception that such activities are beyond their expertise or affordability, and are perhaps considered to be optional academic subjects that are only applicable to larger organisations. Consequently, many of those who are responsible for continuing with business as usual (BAU) may live with the constant fear and the never-ending question of how to protect their business in the event of a disaster, and who would help if such a disaster should occur. This book simplifies the procedures and processes used to successfully implement a workable DR and BC plan. It removes any doubts or uncertainties about how it can be easily achieved with the help of a simple combination of qualified internal members of staff, contractors, external consultants and some common sense.

It provides a short description and explanation of the various DR and BC terms and concepts used. The book draws on the best management practice contained in ISO22301, the latest Standard, to ensure that organisations of any size are able to benefit from its guidance.

Some chapters provide examples of IT and non-IT disasters that could strike an organisation at any time, and may be elaborated on with the use of a fictitious organisation called RockSolid Corp.

Preface

Unless stated otherwise, the names of any companies or people mentioned in any examples are fictitious. Where names of actual companies and products are mentioned, they are the trademarks of their respective organisations.

Thejendra B.S

January 2014

CONTENTS

**Chapter 1: Introduction to Disaster Recovery and
Business Continuity** 1
Who should read this book? 2
What is a disaster? 3
What is disaster recovery (DR)? 6
What is business continuity (BC)? 7
What is Crisis Management? 9
Why are DR and BC important? 10
Who are the real owners of DR, BC, and CM? 12
What is the cost of a disaster? 14
Who are the right persons to manage DR and BC? 16
What is a DR or BC site? 20
What is a command centre? 21
Where should a DR or BC site be located? 21
Can an organisation manage DR and BC alone? 23
What about DR and BC assistance from external
consultants? 26
What kinds of disaster should an organisation be aware
of? 27
What is a technical risk? 29
What are some of the most common technical risks? 30
What are some of the most common non-technical
disasters? 31
What is a business impact analysis (BIA)? 31
Who can invoke BC? 33
What are the options available for BC? 34
What is a DR or BC exercise? 35
What are the biggest roadblocks for DR or BC? 35
What are the costs of establishing a proper DR facility? 36

Contents

Are there any international qualifications or training for DR and BC?........ 38

Are there any international standards for BC planning? 38

Chapter 2: Data Disasters 41

What is data? 41

What is meant by risk to data?......................... 42

Why and how do companies lose data?................. 42

How should organisations store data safely?............... 43

What are some of the most common storage and back-up options?.................. 45

What is meant by Recovery Time Objective (RTO) and Recovery Point Objective (RPO)?................. 47

What is Internet back-up?.............. 48

What is a 'geocluster'? 49

How often should back-ups be taken, and what should be backed up? 49

How can one decide what data needs to be backed-up?. 50

How and where should back-up tapes be stored?.......... 50

How often should back-ups be tested? 51

Will taking proper data back-ups daily ensure DR?....... 52

What is 'disk mirroring'? 54

What is a 'database replication'?................... 54

What does 'server load balancing' mean?................. 55

How can one prevent loss of IT equipment? 55

On-site disaster prevention methods: 57

Chapter 3: Virus Disasters 61

What is a computer virus? 61

How can an organisation protect itself from viruses? 62

What is a worm?.................. 63

What is a Trojan?.................. 64

How can an organisation recover after a virus attack?... 64

How does one update anti-virus software on all machines? 66

Contents

Dos and don'ts regarding viruses 67
What is 'phishing'? 68
What about safety on mobile devices? 68
Chapter 4: Communication System Disasters 71
What are some of the common methods of
communication in organisations? 71
What is a communication failure? 71
What are some of the methods for preventing Local
Area Network failures? 73
What are some methods for preventing WAN
disasters? 74
Dos and don'ts regarding communication systems 76
Chapter 5: Software Disasters 77
What is a software disaster? 77
What is a mission critical application? 78
What are some of the software disasters that can strike
an organisation? 78
What are some of the best practices for software
disaster prevention? 81
Chapter 6: Data Centre Disasters 85
What is a data centre? 85
How should a data centre be built? 86
What are some of the best practices to prevent
disasters inside data centres? 86
Other precautions to prevent IT disasters 88
Chapter 7: IT Staff Member Disasters 91
Who is meant by members of IT staff? 91
What are the general precautions to prevent disasters
relating to members of IT staff? 91
What is an appropriate IT member of staff ratio? 93
What are the usual reasons for members of IT staff
disasters? 95

Contents

What are some of the best practices to be followed by members of IT staff?.. 96

What are the main benefits of using ITIL?.................... 96

How can change management prevent disasters?........... 97

What are the other risks relating to members of IT staff?.. 99

Chapter 8: IT Contractor Disasters 101

What is an IT contractor-related disaster?.................... 101

How can organisations protect themselves against IT vendor-related disasters?.. 102

How does one prevent IT-contractor support disasters?... 102

Should IT staff be outsourced?.................................... 103

What can be outsourced?... 105

Questions to ask vendors 107

Is it necessary to have contracts with vendors?........... 107

What are the key elements of a maintenance contract or an SLA?... 108

Chapter 9: IT Project Failures 113

Why do IT projects fail?... 115

How can organisations avoid IT project failures?........ 117

Chapter 10: Information Security............................ 123

What is information security?....................................... 123

What are the various ways in which information security can be compromised?....................................... 124

What safeguards are available to protect information? 125

Chapter 11: Cyber Security Issues 127

What is Cyber Security?... 127

What is hacking? 128

How can an organisation prevent hacking?.................. 132

Exploring Cloud services... 133

Chapter 12: Introduction to Non-IT Disasters.......... 135

Contents

What are some of the non-IT disasters that could affect an organisation?.................................... 135

What is a human error?.................................... 136

What are marketing and sales errors?.................. 137

What are financial disasters?.......................... 137

What are some of the common recruitment risks?....... 138

How do you handle fire related disasters?............ 139

What about health and biological threats to an organisation's members of staff?..................... 140

What about electrical failures and blackouts?........ 141

What precautions can an organisation take to handle civil disturbances?................................... 143

How can an organisation take precaution against terrorism?.. 143

What is a travel-related risk?....................... 145

What are the usual trade or labour union problems?.... 147

What about the psychological effects of a disaster on members of staff?.................................... 149

What is a reputational risk?......................... 149

What about industrial espionage?..................... 151

How can an organisation prevent a disaster relating to paper documents?.................................... 154

What other precautions can an organisation take?....... 155

Chapter 13: Disaster Recovery at Home 157

What are the main risks associated with home working?... 157

What are some of the ways to prevent disasters occurring in homes?.................................. 158

Document and data management......................... 161

Data back-up for standalone systems 161

Sample recommended solution.......................... 162

Chapter 14: Plenty of Questions...................... 165

Questions on planning and security................... 165

xv

Contents

Questions on technology 166
Questions on health and safety 168
Questions on financial and legal issues 169
Questions on people... 170
Chapter 15: How do I get Started? 173
How does one start a DR or BC programme? 173
How do I create an actual BCP?................................. 178
Common types of plans 179
How is an IT contingency plan prepared?.................. 200
Sample IT contingency plan for a mission critical
server 201
What is a mock run and how is it conducted?............. 205
How often should the DR or BC plan be updated? 207
What should a BC/DR checklist consist of?................. 207
Sample useful checklists... 208
**Appendix 1: Disaster Recovery Training and
Certification.. 219**
Appendix 2: Business Continuity Standards............. 225
ISO22301 225
Appendix 3: Making DR and BC Exciting 227
Appendix 4: Disaster Recovery Glossary 229
ITG Resources.. 275

CHAPTER 1: INTRODUCTION TO DISASTER RECOVERY AND BUSINESS CONTINUITY

'Meet success like a gentleman and disaster like a man.'

Frederick Edwin Smith (1872-1930)

During the last decade, organisations have undergone huge technical and non-technical transformations, and in the last few years the business world has changed significantly. Regardless of the industry, more and more organisations around the world are operating 7 days a week, 24 hours a day. Competition has increased dramatically, and multiple options for a customer's demand are available at the click of a mouse. Even a small organisation with only a few staff members depends on technology to compete globally in order to remain in business, which is of paramount importance to every organisation. It's almost impossible to run any organisation without the use of a computer or telecom-related technology, and this can't be achieved using the same methods and processes that were used five or ten years ago. For example, any organisation today will require computers, databases, internet access, e-mail, web-hosting and telephones for running its business. Furthermore, the advancement in new technology and its ready availability has enabled an organisation to implement and use it to great effect just to continue with business as usual.

Although an organisation may have implemented modern technologies, they may, or may not have the expertise to support them internally. As a result, there is a high dependence on external, qualified contractors and service providers that can provide timely and efficient service for various mission critical IT functions of an organisation.

Today, because of the numerous technical interdependencies that have become a necessity in all areas of business, no organisation is immune to risk. Therefore, preventing, minimising and avoiding the risk of all types of unexpected disaster or threat has become particularly important. Traditional methods of protection may have been by means of an insurance policy. This would provide cover and protection against damage to key equipment, for example, in the event of a fire or flood, or any other event which the policyholder may have opted for. However, today's business needs and requirements demand more than this, or simply *'hoping for the best'*. An organisation has to protect itself from the ever increasing number of physical and virtual threats and risks.

With so much dependence on technology, those responsible are constantly faced with the same questions, such as:

- How can one manage predictable disasters striking an organisation?

- Who is best qualified to protect an organisation?

- What qualifications and mindset does one need to work in a DR and BC department?

- Where and how can one find or identify such people?

Who should read this book?

This book is aimed at anyone who is directly or indirectly involved with disaster recovery or business continuity. If you belong to one of the groups mentioned below then you will find this book extremely useful. Though the book is aimed at small and medium organisations the concepts hold good for large organisations too.

- IT managers
- Chief technical officers or chief information officers
- Business managers and consultants
- Board members
- Risk and safety officers
- IT consultants
- Anyone who has been assigned the responsibility for overseeing DR and BC for their organisation.

What is a disaster?

A disaster is generally considered to be *'an occurrence causing widespread destruction and distress, or a catastrophe'*. In a business environment, any event or crisis that adversely affects or disables an organisation's ability to continue with business as usual is a disaster.

According to various surveys and studies conducted by agencies like DRJ (Disaster Recovery Journal) and Forrester Research, many organisations worldwide go out of business every year because of a disaster - many of which were fully preventable. Many small organisations are often unable to recover from a major disaster, and even larger organisations may find it difficult. As a result, it is vital that organisations constantly minimise all predictable and controllable risks and ensure that they have a properly tested disaster recovery plan in place, should an event occur. A disaster recovery plan is now a mandatory audit and compliance requirement in many organisations. Naturally, organisations won't be able to safeguard themselves against all types of disasters, but they can definitely prevent and safeguard their business against many of the more common types.

Disasters can occur in a variety of forms, as demonstrated by the following examples. As mentioned earlier, a fictitious company called RockSolid Corp is used in many examples throughout this book.

Example 1 – Natural disaster

Due to a mishap, there was a serious fire in RockSolid's computer data centre and all of the mission critical computers that contained years of business data, together with any required business applications, were destroyed. This would automatically mean that most of the organisation's members of staff would be unable to continue with their work, and within a small amount of time the whole organisation could come to a standstill, because it is unable to continue with 'business as usual'. For an organisation to recover from such a disaster, it would require a huge amount of time, cost and effort. However, although some losses may be measurable, other losses also have to be considered, which perhaps may not be so easily measured, for example, damage to an organisation's reputation.

Example 2 – Technical disaster

A hacker intrusion into an organisation's computers can result in a serious technical fault, such as a deadly virus attack or a software bug that causes all of its computers to shut down.

Example 3 – Lack of knowledge

Finance Department: 'Hello. Our finance server is not working. Can you fix it?'

Help desk: 'Which one?'

Finance Department: 'The one that we use in our department. It's a black system with a green keyboard.'

Help desk: 'I had a look at it, but the hard disk is dead and we will have to replace it. I will call the vendor and arrange for a replacement if possible.'

Finance Department: 'What about our data?'

Help desk: 'I'm afraid we can't recover the data. The disk is dead and we have not been backing up the data of that server, because nobody told us to. Finance did not approve the purchase of a tape drive for this machine.'

Finance Department: 'Oh no. We have our entire payroll, purchasing, billing, sales and other important financial data for the entire company on that machine. Five years of data!'

Help desk: 'Unfortunately there is nothing we can do. Please excuse me, I have to go and attend another call.'

A situation like that can cripple your organisation within hours.

To summarise, in no time at all, an organisation can inflict serious damage to its business simply through lack of adequate knowledge, or by having a *'penny wise, pound foolish'* way of thinking.

And there are other types of potential disaster. Some disasters could even be deliberate, such as, sabotage, theft, or espionage.

What is disaster recovery (DR)?

Computer systems and networks are extremely complex and complicated, and in view of this and the inter-dependencies of various equipment, processes and people, etc., a disaster can strike anywhere at any time. The current business environment is highly competitive, and the days when an organisation could resume business as usual at its leisure; that is, within a few days or weeks, are over.

If a mission critical computer system is not working, or unavailable, then in no time at all an organisation may be unable to continue with its business as usual. Therefore, it must be able to quickly resume its mission critical business functions from almost the exact point in time that the disaster struck, because it's almost impossible to switch over to an alternative manual or legacy process for any length of time. Although global awareness of DR and BC is increasing, very few organisations are well enough equipped and prepared to respond to a disaster and quickly continue with its business as usual functions.

1: Introduction to Disaster Recovery and Business Continuity

DR is the methodical planning, preparation and execution of all the steps in the process that will be needed to recover from a disaster quickly. It is mainly *technology-focused*, for example, voice and data communication systems, servers and computers, databases, critical data, web servers and e-mail. A DR plan should have tested and proven methods to tackle and recover from all predictable and controllable IT disasters for each of the pre-mentioned examples and more. If there is a mission critical server running critical software, then a DR plan for the server could be a 'standby' that's located elsewhere and running the identical software with daily data synchronization. In addition, the main system can also have disk mirroring, tape back-ups, a periodic image back-up and proper change management processes, for added precautions.

Well implemented DR is of critical importance to an organisation. It should be documented and periodically updated with details of the contact information for key members of staff, the locations of back-ups, recovery procedures, vendor and contractor information, contracts, communications procedures, and a testing schedule. Additional elements may be necessary depending on the size of an organisation. Further information can be found on this in *Chapter 15*.

What is business continuity (BC)?

BC ensures that an organisation's mission critical business functions can continue to operate regardless of a disaster striking. It is a process that identifies various risks or threats to an organisation, and provides responsive measures to safeguard the interests of its key stakeholders, customers, reputation, brand value, etc. Should a disaster strike, the natural approach would be to deploy all critical members of staff to concentrate their effort on making a recovery; which may be done within a matter of minutes, hours or days - or not at all. However, in many customer focused organisations; in parallel to responding to a disaster, it's also essential to ensure that certain '*minimum*' business functions '*continue*' to operate regardless. BC is mainly *business-focused* and will concentrate on strategies and plans in the event of a disaster. It will prepare organisations and their business areas to survive serious business interruptions, and provide the ability to perform certain mission critical business functions - even during a disruptive event. For example, if a major disaster strikes the main mission critical computer system of a bank during banking hours, a quick decision can be made to continue with business as usual. This could be by allowing customers to continue depositing and withdrawing a nominal amount of cash until the problem is fixed. This is BC. It ensures that customers have a minimal acceptable service in spite of a disaster, and also helps preserve the bank's reputation and image etc.

Note: A BC solution need not always require a technical solution for a technical disaster. It's about providing quick workable alternatives to minimise adverse impact. Anything that meets the purpose can be classified as BC. Business continuity management (BCM) is managing risks to ensure that mission critical functions continue to provide an acceptable level of service, even in the event of a major IT or non-IT disaster. If, for example, the entire data centre that housed all of the important servers was damaged by a fire, electrical short circuit, or some other unexpected disaster, the BCM team should be able to assist in recovering the organisation from such situations using pre-planned methods - BC planning (BCP). It should prepare an organisation for DR actions that apply before, if, or when a disaster occurs.

If budgets and resources were unlimited, it's probable that an entire organisation could be duplicated elsewhere. However, such luxury is rarely available, nor practical. The final decision of the appropriate BC action that should be implemented in response to each type of disaster should be made in consultation with a number of departments and business managers. As previously stated, a BC method need not always require a technical solution. The BCM team must be able to provide cost-effective and acceptable disaster prevention solutions to each mission critical business function.

What is Crisis Management?

Depending on the nature of a disaster, it may be necessary for an organisation to convene a group of senior managers to, for example, control adverse media reports, manage customer satisfaction, or retain deserting customers. This is crisis management. It is also panic prevention, and its function becomes important to protect an organisation from a disaster such as negative and exaggerated media reports, that may cause widespread panic and have an adverse impact on it, for example, its stock price, or reputation. In the event of a major disaster, a crisis management team can ensure that such situations and possibilities are controlled by taking proactive action to minimise the impact, and therefore its losses.

Table 1: Summary and examples of concepts

Disaster	A bank's mission critical computer fails during peak banking hours. Critical business functions are halted - cashiers are unable to verify account balances, or conduct electronic transactions.
Disaster Recovery (DR)	Members of IT can repair the computer by replacing the hard disk and restoring data as fast as possible. However, this could take several hours or more than a day.
Business Continuity (BC)	Bank management decide to allow customers to make transactions manually, using 'withdrawal' and 'paying-in' slips.
Crisis management (CM)	Senior executives of the bank assure customers that the technical problem won't cause any financial loss or improper accounting to anyone.

Note: Although the academic definitions and meanings of DR and BC are different, this book uses both terms in parallel, so the answers and concepts hold good for both in many cases.

Why are DR and BC important?

Many organisations have become extremely dependent on technology for their business as usual operations, and to provide a service to their customers. An important concern is that any major damage to an organisation's infrastructure can result in severe financial losses, loss of reputation, and may even result in its closure. This is because it can be extremely difficult and complex for an organisation to switch over to manual processes for any length of time during a business interruption. For example, it isn't possible to revert to manual typewriters, telex and hand-written documents if the whole computer system, Internet and e-mail network is down. Many are also internally and externally inter-connected via the Internet, hence any technology-related failures external to the organisation can result in it being globally isolated. Some of the reasons why DR and BC are important for an organisation are as follows:

- Organisations have become extremely dependent on IT. As a result, IT failures are more likely to affect an organisation than failures in other areas, of its business, and the impact of such a failure is more likely to be severe.

- In a networked, workflow type of environment, a failure can affect many departments and units.

- IT environments have become extremely complex and inter-related, so the number of potential failure points is increasing all the time.

- In the event of an IT failure, there isn't enough time to recover 'at one's leisure', because of end-user, customer and other business pressures.

- Without a proven DR and BC process an organisation could go out of business very quickly.

Who are the real owners of DR, BC, and CM?

This is actually a tricky question. An organisation may have employed its own members of IT staff, or external contractors to provide technical support and operate a critical server. Many would assume the real owners are the staff supporting the IT equipment, or the operators handling the business functions, because they operate the system, and as such, understand how it works. However, this is an incorrect assumption. The real owners are the organisation's business managers, because if the main server stops operating, the members of IT staff can't be held responsible for the organisation failing to continue with business as usual. They may know what it takes to repair or restore the system, but it's the business managers who should know and understand the big picture, such as the impact that the potential loss of any mission critical business and IT functions can have on the organisation, that is, in terms of financial, reputational and legalities. Hence, the business managers are the real owners of DR, BC and CM, and as such, are responsible for ensuring that the necessary budgets, manpower, resources and alternative methods are in place to tackle and prevent a disaster. Some of the ways in which an organisation's business managers can demonstrate ownership are as follows:

- **Knowledge:** Understand the financial, reputational, regulatory or legal impact that a disaster can have on an organisation's mission critical business function, or IT equipment.

- **Financial support:** Provide the necessary budgets for comprehensive maintenance, such as, hardware, software, telecom equipment, spares, and back-up devices. For example, if an organisation's business manager declines to approve the purchase of equipment or necessary software that is of an acceptable standard of quality, or fail to enter into a hardware maintenance contract agreement for an important server, then members of IT staff won't be able to take the relevant appropriate action in the event of a server crash, data loss or other technical problem that may occur.

- **Manpower:** Ensure that departments have the necessary resources in all areas. It is common for an organisation to have insufficient manpower to provide support and maintenance, but nevertheless demand the best from an under-resourced workforce. The common saying *'Hire an Einstein, but refuse his request for a blackboard'* describes a situation that is prevalent in many organisations worldwide. Reduced manpower and facilities in critical areas will inevitably, directly or indirectly, affect the organisation. (Member of staff ratios will be covered in more detail later in the book).

- **Implement recommendations:** Establishing DR and BC is an expensive business. Listen to recommendations proposed by members of IT and support staff for implementing DR and BC environments. Not every critical IT function can be worked around with a low-cost alternative. It is common practice in many organisations to ignore, or avoid IT and non-IT recommendations - using cost as an excuse. If an organisation is serious about implementing DR and BC, then senior management must provide support in terms of the necessary costs and budgets for implementing all sensible recommendations, industry standards and workarounds necessary, even though a disaster may never strike.

- **Be involved:** Senior management at all levels must get involved in all aspects of an organisation's DR and BC processes, and adopt a *'Show me'* or *'Prove it to me'* attitude to ensure its business is truly protected. It is a mandatory business and audit requirement for many organisations to have a BC or DR site, which is an alternative site that can be used if the primary or main site fails or becomes inaccessible.

- **Policies:** As with other essential policies, such as, in human resources (HR), or finance, a DR and BC policy must be enforced for all critical systems by senior management.

- **Sustained commitment:** DR and BC is a continuous exercise, and it's worth remembering that its facilities are similar to insurance, that is, they are a constant expense. It isn't enough to show an interest and invest on a one-off basis, because establishing proper DR and BC facilities requires continuous commitment and expenditure.

What is the cost of a disaster?

A disaster can lead to substantial costs, implications and long-term damage; not only in terms of the financial cost, such as the equipment or process that's failed, but possibly many other hidden costs and issues. It can even have long-term cascading affects, and depending on the nature of the organisation's business the various costs associated with a disaster could include the following:

- loss of business
- loss of reputation

- loss of customers

- stock prices falling or free-fall

- reduced staff productivity

- billing costs

- unnecessary expenditure

- fines and penalties - regulatory

- lawsuits

- travel and logistics expenses

- insurance and other associated miscellaneous costs

- other industry-specific losses.

Business costs: This is the anticipated loss of money that an organisation would have lost if its systems weren't working. For example, if its business is operated via a website, such as Amazon.com, it could lose thousands of pounds an hour in revenue to its competition for each hour that its website was down.

Productivity costs: This is calculated using the number of affected members of staff, and multiplying this by their hourly cost. For example, if an organisation hired ten external consultants at £100 an hour to develop software on a server, and that server was down for three hours, it would incur a loss of £3,000. This is because the amount will still have to be paid to the consultants without any productive work in return.

Reputation costs: No specific formula exists to calculate the costs of an organisation's reputation. It can range from a minor manageable scratch, to a total crash of its share value and image to customers and the general public. For example, if an organisation's purchase order system is down, resulting in a delay of orders beyond committed delivery dates, it runs the risk of losing those orders to its competitors, or suffers reputational damage due to not fulfilling them in time.

Direct costs: Costs for repair or replacement of the failed equipment, manpower costs, contractor costs, or liabilities.

Other costs: Costs specific to an organisation, for example, as a result of a customer taking legal action for a delay.

Depending on the disaster, one or more of the above losses could ruin an organisation, demonstrating the importance of paying due attention to DR and BC practices and processes. Each of the above costs should be considered in sufficient detail, and the probability of an occurrence must be calculated to ensure proper BC alternatives. Any damage must be estimated in terms of, for example, revenue, reputation, security and members of staff. Based on this calculation, a detailed BC plan should be prepared and implemented to ensure that its business activities can resume following a disruption.

Who are the right persons to manage DR and BC?

An organisation's business managers may argue that DR and BC are now almost a mature science, with numerous consultants, templates, certifications and best practices available to everyone. If an organisation has a requirement to set-up DR and BC, there are many suitably qualified and competent professionals available to carry out the role. However, the ideal candidates to manage a DR and/or BC function will still need some special skills that training

programmes or certification are usually unable to teach -
and they need to be of a very different mindset.

Skill 1: Nature of a pessimist

The most suitable person to carry out the role in an
organisation's DR and BC department is one who is able to
think, speak and plan as a pessimist, and constantly spreads
a healthy dose of pessimism. Every organisation that's
serious about risk management should nurture, promote and
respect such an individual in order to protect its business
from any risks they may face.

It's easy to dispute why an organisation should have a
requirement for a pessimist, and it's unlikely that a statue
has ever been erected in honour of one. Most people insist
on the need for brave leaders, such as those who are able to
make tough decisions, are flamboyant and able to lead and
boldly take the less travelled road. This wouldn't be
expected of a pessimist. Braveness, toughness and other
leadership skills are required to run and grow an
organisation, but those whose thinking is 'out of the box'
are often not suitable for protecting it, because of what they
are, and what they don't want to be.

Investing in a pessimist could be the best business decision
taken to save an organisation from a disaster. A Chinese
proverb says, '*Only a coward can create the best defences*'.
This method should be an approach to protecting an
organisation. A brave person doesn't usually make the
effort to create many defences, because of the self-belief
and confidence of having the power and strength to
withstand and tackle any danger. However, this person is
incapable of seeing risks in the same way that a pessimist is
able to, or of demonstrating the ability to identify the

numerous risks and dangers that exist in practically anything. A pessimist is constantly aware of the numerous dangers that exist and cannot be tackled and therefore, responds by building the best possible defences. This can benefit an organisation, because this person is able to smell and see a risk in an instant, just as a shark is able to smell blood from miles away.

Pessimists have a unique and special advantage by having no limits in their ability to identify risks and things that an ordinary person can't. Pessimists think in an extremely paranoid fashion and fear controls their imagination. They trust no one, not even themselves, and have an '*I will believe it when I see it*' and '*Prove it to me*' attitude. They don't believe anything they have not personally seen working to their absolute satisfaction, and can get into nit-picking detail by viewing risks in numerous ways.

For a pessimist, everything is a risk. Fear helps a pessimist build fantastic fences. A brave leader will not hesitate to go to war, but a pessimist will prevent war from happening as long as possible, or forever. In an organisation, a brash and brave manager may take a quick decision to lay-off a critical member of staff over a trivial matter, whereas, a pessimist may think of how the incident could affect the organisation, what safeguards are currently available, and how the situation could worsen. A pessimist thinks in terms of possible lawsuits, any influential contacts the member of staff may have, or the damage that the aggrieved person could inflict on the organisation.

Skill 2: Leave no important task unfinished

Another important skill a DR or BC professional must have is to leave no task unfinished as explained in a popular farm hand story.

Example

A young man applied for a job as a farm-hand. When the farmer asked for his qualifications, he said, *'I can sleep when the wind blows'*. This puzzled the farmer, but he liked the young man and hired him nonetheless.

A few days later, the farmer and his wife were awakened in the night by a violent storm. They quickly began to check things out to see if all was secure. They found that the shutters of the farmhouse had been securely fastened. A good supply of logs had been set next to the fireplace. And the young man slept soundly. The farmer and his wife then inspected their property. They found that the farm tools had been placed in the storage shed, safe from the elements. The tractor had been moved into the garage. The harvest was already stored inside. There was drinking water in the kitchen. The barn was properly locked. Even the animals were calm. All was well. It was only then that the farmer understood the meaning of the young man's words, *'I can sleep when the wind blows'*. Since the farmhand did his work loyally and faithfully when the skies were clear, he was prepared for the storm when it broke. And when the wind blew, he was not afraid. He could sleep in peace. And, indeed, he was sleeping in peace.

Moral of the story?

There was nothing dramatic or sensational in the young farm-hand's preparations. He just faithfully did what was needed each day. The story illustrates a principle that is often overlooked about being prepared for various events that occur in life. It is only when we are facing the weather that

---

we wish we had taken care of certain things that needed attention much earlier.

What is a DR or BC site?

The terms DR and BC site are sometimes used interchangeably. Either way, it is usually an alternative site that can be used by an organisation if the primary or main site fails, or becomes inaccessible. For example, if an organisation is struck by a major IT disaster that prevents its members of staff from providing critical technical support on various financial applications to a key external client. In response to DR, certain support staff can immediately relocate to the DR or BC site, start providing technical support and continue to do so while the main site is being fixed. The site must of course have the necessary IT infrastructure and facilities to provide the required minimum, or mutually agreed level of support.

Depending on the size of an organisation or its importance, a DR or BC site can be any or all of the following:

- A small or fully-fledged alternative workable office with essential technical set-up in the same location.

- A small or fully-fledged alternative workable site with essential technical set-up at a different location, that is in a different state, or even a different country.

- A branch office where essential functions can continue.

- An outsourced location provided by a third party service provider. Many organisations provide generic or custom-made locations for other organisations for a fee.

- Certain activities can also be carried out from home if remote connectivity options are available.

What is a command centre?

A command centre is a facility with an adequate means of communication, for example, telephones, internet availability and other basic facilities required to begin recovery operations. Typically, it is a temporary facility used by senior management, or those tasked to begin coordinating the recovery process until the alternative sites are functional.

Where should a DR or BC site be located?

Several factors need to be considered when establishing where a DR or BC site should be located, It depends on the nature of the organisation's business and its dependent items, for example, its contractor services, communication links and material availabilities. Also, consideration should be given to any political, geographical, natural, human or any other risks which may be associated with its location. For example, a software development organisation that is heavily dependent on international telecom links should not have its site located in a remote area where telecom contractors are unable to provide data and voice links. On the contrary, a small manufacturing organisation, for example, could probably have its site fitted with some essential equipment, located anywhere that has an electrical supply and transport facilities. Basic communication can be done using mobile phones or laptops connected with wireless internet.

From a logistics perspective, if essential services are to continue quickly, it is sensible to have an alternative DR or

BC site located reasonably near the main site to avoid long travel times and associated logistics problems. Travelling time is a key factor to consider when deciding on the location of a site. Other factors to consider are as follows:

* Data transfer requirements between both sites.

* Periodicity and amount of data.

* Ease of travel between both sites.

* Availability of support services, for example telecom contractors, computer contractors and spare parts.

* Availability of essential facilities, such as power and water. It is also preferable to have the site powered by a different electrical power grid to that of the main site.

* Political and civil issues at the location. For example, it does not make sense to set up the site at a location that may suffer periodic civil and political disturbances.

* Some organisations prefer to locate their sites in other countries. For example, many software development companies in India have a site in Singapore which operates in parallel, synchronizing its data. Therefore, if a disaster was to strike the main site in India, a core essential team in Singapore can continue with business as usual and keep their data intact.

Establishing and maintaining a ready-to-use DR or BC site can be an expensive business. Fortunately the need to use it may never occur, but as with an insurance policy, one can never predict when it will be necessary.

Can an organisation manage DR and BC alone?

DR and BC is not rocket science. In fact, it is common sense to ensure that an organisation does not suffer as a result of factors that are within its control. However, its planning must be developed with the effort of several departments. Although an individual in a small organisation may oversee it, it's not an individual effort. The person best suited to carry out the role of a DR or BC manager is one that is paranoid and worries about anything and everything, but is still able to communicate. Before developing a plan, every organisation must classify its functions in terms of priorities and impacts. Business and technical managers must analyse the business together, and rank it in terms of priorities and business impact. For example, an organisation may classify all of its business functions as low, medium and high priorities, with a business impact for each. Obviously, not everything carried out by an organisation can be classified as high priority or high impact.

Questions to support classification could include:

- What business functions must be up and running within minutes or hours in the event of a disaster striking? For example, an organisation that is highly dependent on e-mail for its business cannot afford to have its server down. Therefore, it may classify e-mail as high priority, thereby taking all necessary steps to have an alternative e-mail system in place. Whereas, an organisation that depends heavily on a web server may classify all its web systems as high priority.

- What business functions can be down for 24 hours? An organisation that depends occasionally on facsimiles may classify its facsimile services as medium priority, because it can tolerate a day's downtime.

- What business functions can be down for more than 24 hours, more than two days, or a week? Certain software development projects and product development that are still in the design or development stage may be able to tolerate a few days or weeks of downtime and as a result classify it as a low priority.

Successful running of a DR or BC site may also depend on other factors. If an organisation has several experienced members of staff who are familiar with the details of all of the business processes, that is, how they work and their importance, then it is possible for them to develop fairly good DR or BC planning. Alternatives are the use of external consultants, or the use of standard templates. Templates are detailed prepared checklists that compare an organisation's preparation. For example, a fire department may provide a template or checklist that provides details of checks for fire prevention. It is also possible to have a building inspected by a fire department to certify whether it's safe or not. Similarly, a back-up software manufacturer can provide a checklist of the important things to take into account both during, and after a backup of data.

Important tip: Anything within an organisation's control must get the necessary priority, budgets and importance. The following checklist can be used:

- What areas and business functions are *completely* within an organisation's control? Computers, data and back-ups are usually within an organisation's control for recovery. Any loss here can be handled by the organisation by implementing various safeguards and budgets, using its own manpower and resources.

- What areas and business functions are *partially* within an organisation's control? There could be some dependence on an external service provider, such as a telephone network that is provided by a telecommunication organisation. It cannot have its own independent telephone network that is separate from the external world — it's dependent on local and international telecommunication service providers. Problems and loss of service by the service provider can affect an organisation's business, but will not be within its control. However, if it is unable to use landlines, perhaps mobile phones can be used temporarily until the telecom department fixes the fault.

- What areas and business functions are *outside* of the organisation's control? For example, if an office is located in close vicinity of an oil or gas terminal, and a fire occurs within those facilities, it can affect the organisation's buildings and any others nearby. Or, in the event of a terrorist attack, the police may cordon off the whole area, thus prevent members of staff from travelling to and from the workplace. Senior management will have no say or control in such matters, but will simply have to cooperate regardless of the loss of business. In such an event, an organisation may have to resort to an insurance claim, an alternative site, delays, etc.

What about DR and BC assistance from external consultants?

Nowadays, DR consultancy itself is a big business, and many consultants and consultancy firms have sprung up all over the world claiming to be the best of them all. It's also industry-specific. However, it isn't possible to get a single, good DR consultancy that covers the entire range of business and technical processes; even though they may all claim to be experts in every area. It is necessary to evaluate the need for inviting external consultants, and then decide the way forward. In most cases, a combination of internal and external expertise would be appropriate.

The best consultants to start the process could already be within an organisation. An experienced professional knowledgeable of the requirements in the event of a disaster striking their area of work, together with a combination of internal experienced members of staff, and external consultants would be a good choice. An organisation must select DR consultants carefully, and avoid those who only give superficial advice. However, it may not be easy to pin-point a single consultant for all business needs, but to make a choice based on the area of DR coverage. Credentials and references play an important role in selection, for example, hire a reputable, or experienced IT person to recommend IT DR methods and a reputable financial consultant to provide financial DR methods.

Ideally, a DR or BC consultant must be a '*nuts and bolts*' person, that is, someone who can sit with key members of staff to understand the needs and requirements, so as to recommend practical real-world solutions. If an organisation requires a DR facility for its financial systems, the consultant should sit with the finance team and gain an understanding of how the system works, together with the software, type of equipment and data synchronization that's required. This should be undertaken before recommending a suitable DR setup, and the consultant must be able to demonstrate its working with a mock run.

The importance of practical experience: Sir Francis Bacon said long ago, *'Knowledge is power'*. Perhaps this can be modified for today's world as *'Practical knowledge is power'*. Although professional certifications are becoming very important in any role, practical and real-world knowledge is of paramount importance. It is also important to *'first learn the trade before experimenting with tricks of the trade'*. Practical, hands-on experience and implementation ability are the keys to good DR consultancy.

What kinds of disaster should an organisation be aware of?

Disasters can come in all shapes and forms and be internal or external. Therefore, different factors need to be considered for each critical system. All of an organisation's processes and systems should be classified into broad categories and tackled one at a time. The DR or BC selection process starts with an assessment of the potential risks and their probability and impact for a particular enterprise. Next is a business impact analysis (BIA). This helps to determine which applications and systems require the most protection. This is based on the value of the data and the business impact of downtime, as well as other cost factors. Some of the common types of risks are,

- **Technical risks:** This will cover all IT-related issues, such as, including back-ups, data storage and retrieval, loss of equipment, communication failures, virus attacks, software problems and power failures.

- **Non-technical risks:** Building security, theft, fire hazards and access by unauthorised personnel.

- **Financial and legal risks:** Stock market manipulation, bankruptcy, fraud, financial irregularities, failure to comply with legal regulations or standards.

- **Human risks:** Loss of important members of key staff to competitors, or resignations, death, injury, illness, disgruntlement, workplace harassment and industrial espionage.

- **Reputational risks:** All factors that can affect an organisation's image, for example, harassment of members of staff, litigation, legal turmoil and bad publicity.

- **Dependency risks:** If an organisation depends on external companies, contractors and even other countries for its business, it could be at risk. For example, a restaurant that is dependent on the existence of a large organisation nearby may go out of business if that organisation relocates.

- **Natural risks:** Fire, flood, earthquake and hurricane.

- **Political risks:** Change of government and policies, civil disturbances and terrorism.

An organisation can broadly classify risks with their probability of occurrence and impact, as follows:

Table 2: Simple risk analysis

RISK	PROBABILITY	IMPACT
Technical	High	High
Political	Low	High
Financial	Medium	High
Fire	High	High

Note: DR and BC is an ongoing process. It can *never* be perfect or complete.

What is a technical risk?

An organisation will use one or more of the following IT systems:

- Computers of various sizes and capacities ranging from small laptops to large mainframes.

- Data back-up systems to store and retrieve large amounts of data.

- E-mail systems for internal and external communication.

- Telecommunication systems, for example, facsimile, dial-up lines, mobile phones, leased lines for connecting offices, branches between different geographical locations.

- Various software programmes, for example, office suites, databases, remote connectivity tools, monitoring tools, design software and e-mail.

- Website servers for hosting intranets and public servers.

... and potentially dozens of other enterprise technologies.

Each of the above must be interconnected if an organisation is to function, but each has the potential to fail in a number of areas. A simple cable disconnection on an international data leased line can cut off every part of an entire organisation. Heavy usage of any such equipment always entails a hidden risk. Similarly, any item of equipment can fail in its own unique way, or behave erratically for various reasons. For example, if the power supply fluctuates there is a high probability of computer disks crashing, or corruption of data on many computers. All such IT-related failures, or potential failures can be classified as technical risks, and sufficient workable cost-effective alternatives are needed to minimise risk.

What are some of the most common technical risks?

Some of the most common technical risks to an organisation are listed below, and will be covered in more detail in later chapters. Risks that can range from simple problems to absolute catastrophes are as follows:

- Risk to data
- Virus risks
- Power failure risks
- Local area network (LAN) failures
- Information security risks
- Telecommunication risks.

What are some of the most common non-technical disasters?

Some of the most common non-technical disasters and risks that an organisation may face are as follows:

- Members of IT staff
- IT contractors
- Reputation
- Financial
- Labour union
- Legal
- Political
- Natural
- Terrorist.

Most of these will be covered in a separate chapter on non-IT disasters – *see Chapter 12.*

What is a business impact analysis (BIA)?

This is a detailed analysis of the impact on an organisation if a specific set of IT or non-IT services aren't available. Its purpose is to determine the risks, for example, in terms of loss of revenue, reputation or productivity if an IT infrastructure or other mission critical facility is down due to a disaster. A BIA will consider the impact of the following:

- Damage to premises or data centre.

- Damage to IT systems, such as servers, computers, networks or telecommunications.

- Damage to important data in terms of loss or corruption.

- Loss of key members of staff, such as IT support or business managers.

- External and internal customers if a disaster occurred.

- Legal and reputational implications if a disaster occurred.

- Dependencies on external contractors and suppliers.

- Security threats, for example viruses and hackers who may steal confidential information.

- Damage and loss of power, air conditioners, etc., required for IT services.

- Damage due to, for example, sabotage, natural disasters and political threats.

- Other industry-specific impacts.

An example, of a very basic BIA could be as follows:

Table 3: Simple business impact analysis

System	Probability	Impact of downtime
Organisation web server down	High	£5,000 in lost business per hour
Organisation local	Medium	Productivity loss of

network down		£50 per hour, per member of staff

Organisations could prepare similar tables to decide which critical business functions require priority in a business continuity plan (BCP).

Who can invoke BC?

As part of a BCP an organisation must first decide what qualifies as a disaster. Any routine equipment problem, maintenance downtime and short-term problem should not be termed as a disaster, thus invoking alternative facilities. The decision to brand an IT shutdown as a disaster must be taken only by the organisation's senior management and IT managers. A business recovery team can also be constituted: this is a group of qualified senior members of staff responsible for maintaining the business recovery procedures, and for coordinating the recovery of the organisation's critical business functions. For example, if an entire IT infrastructure is out of action as a result of power failure, but the failure is expected to be rectified within a short period of time, then the organisation need not classify it as a disaster, thereby invoking its DR or BC plan. On the other hand, if it is ascertained that the power failure is more severe, and can't be restored within a timescale that is deemed acceptable, then the senior management may invoke the DR procedures.

The following types of disaster can necessitate invoking BC beyond the agreed recovery time objective (RTO) and recovery point objective (RPO) (explained in *Chapter 2*):

- Severe or major business impact to an organisation
- Adverse customer impact

- High risk exposure to organisation

- Critical system down.

What are the options available for BC?

Technically and financially it's possible to build a duplicate of an organisation, but not everyone may want this, or can afford such a luxury. BC is industry-specific. For example, the emergency services like the police or ambulance may not be able to afford to have their IT and other infrastructure out of action even for a few minutes, whereas a small car parts manufacturer may be able to withstand it for quite some time. Therefore, depending on the size of an organisation, the nature of its business and its budget, there are a number of options as follows:

Manual: The use of manual methods if possible.

Other offices: If it is decentralised and has many independent branches, then it may be possible to use their facilities until the affected branch comes online again.

Cold standby: It may have an alternative site with basic IT and non-IT facilities that can be used during extended failures.

Warm standby: This requires re-establishing mission critical systems and services within a short period of time - usually achieved by having redundant equipment that can be used in the event of a disaster.

Hot standby: This requires an alternative site that has continuous mirroring of live data and configurations. This option is usually used by banks and the military, or if there is no downtime tolerance.

What is a DR or BC exercise?

A way of testing the DR 'readiness' of an organisation is to conduct frequent mock exercises of the various areas included in the DR plan - usually by simulating a crisis situation. Such mock exercises test an organisation's ability to respond to a disaster in a planned and effective manner instead of becoming chaotic. For example, if the finance department server is a mission critical DR item, a mock exercise could be conducted at the weekend, or after normal working hours, by invoking a mock disaster. Such a disaster may involve shutting down the system and relocating the finance team to the DR site. All issues should be recorded, and any limitations, deficiencies, or any missed out items should be noted. The exercises will provide first-hand experience of an organisation's ability to cope and manage in the event of a real disaster. Follow on action may then be taken to ensure a better or more effective DR. For example, if an issue was raised that it isn't possible to operate the finance application without connecting at least one printer, then this should be a follow up action prior to the next exercise.

What are the biggest roadblocks for DR or BC?

Every organisation would like to have 100% DR and BC. However, very few organisations are actually willing to make the necessary investments in terms of resources and costs to ensure reliable DR and BC environments. Some of the biggest roadblocks that prevent proper DR and BC are as follows:

- **Lack of sustained management commitment:** A primary roadblock for DR will be lack of sustained commitment. For example, senior management may approve the establishment of a DR or BC site at a time when they are particularly influenced by business and competitive pressures, but may not be willing to invest in the necessary ongoing cost and resources to keep the site fully operational at all times.

- **Inadequate budgets:** Business managers are unable, or unwilling, to invest sufficiently to establish DR and BC options. DR options require investment in redundant equipment, spares, data synchronization equipment, software, hardware, training, insurance and alternative sites.

- **Manpower:** Lack of willingness to invest in additional technically qualified members of staff that are required to maintain and manage a DR site.

- **Knowledge:** Lack of knowledge about what is required to establish proper DR.

- **Other reasons:** Various internal factors, office politics, and limitations.

It is a fact that, in many cases, DR and BC plans simply remain on paper, or have insufficient capability to handle real disasters. If an organisation is to ensure that it's protected from preventable disasters, it needs to invest in the necessary costs and resources.

What are the costs of establishing a proper DR facility?

The costs of establishing a proper DR facility depend on various factors and the nature of the organisation, but generally they can be classified as follows:

- **People:** The number of additional members of staff, contractors and trained members of staff.

- **IT:** The number of additional computer systems, software licences, telephones and communication systems.

- **Maintenance and ongoing:** It isn't enough to simply establish a fully-fledged DR plan as a one-off exercise. It must be properly maintained and periodically updated with new systems, software, data updates, dry runs, etc.

- **Infrastructure and other:** Building rent, electricity, air conditioning, security, transport, telephone.

- **Other costs:** Various one-off or ongoing.

Some dos and don'ts

Do

- Identify a dedicated team within an organisation to be responsible for DR and BC.

- Ensure each member of a DR and BC team understands their role. Clearly establish the scope of DR and BC plans.

- Analyse all business functions and arrange them in order of importance.

- Develop an in-house policy to enforce DR and BC best practices.

- Hold periodic meetings on DR issues and regularly update the DRP.

- Keep customers and members of staff up to date and informed.

- Conduct regular DR mock exercises. Keep up to date with new regulatory requirements, industry practices, standards and qualifications.

Don't

- Take DR and BC functions lightly.

- Give DR inadequate budgets and resources.

- Ignore an organisation's internal talent and knowledge

Are there any international qualifications or training for DR and BC?

More and more employers are looking at certification as a condition of employment. Therefore, because it's often a qualifying pre-requisite for hiring consultants, many universities and institutions have started to provide diploma and graduate courses on DR and BC. There are primarily two recognised professional institutions certifying the BC professional: The Business Continuity Institute (BCI, *www.thebci.org*) based in the UK, and the Disaster Recover Institute International (DRII, *www.drii.org*) based in the USA. Both are member-owned, not-for-profit organisations that offer certification at different levels.

Are there any international standards for BC planning?

ISO22301:2012 (ISO22301) Business Continuity Management Systems (BCSMS) – Requirements is the International Standard for Business Continuity. Launched in May 2012 it replaced the British Standard BS25999-2 and set outs the requirements for a Business Continuity Management System (BCMS). ISO22301 is based on the 'Plan-Do-Check-Act' model as found in other management system standards. An accredited certification scheme exists that enables an organisation to achieve external certification of their BC arrangements.

CHAPTER 2: DATA DISASTERS

'There's no disaster that can't become a blessing, and no blessing that can't become a disaster.'

Richard Bach

This chapter deals with the various ways in which an organisation's data can be exposed to risk and the possible prevention methods.

What is data?

Data is generally defined as *'factual information, especially information organised for analysis or used to reason or make decisions'*. An organisation may have various kinds of data in various formats, for example, important finance documents in Microsoft® Excel® spreadsheets, computer files in Microsoft® Word® documents, databases, e-mails, information on members of staff and customer details. Different organisations view data with varying importance. For example, a credit card supplier will consider the details of the cards numbers as extremely important data, whereas, another organisation may view its technical information, such as software codes and the tools they develop as important. Irrespective of what the specific data is, it's of paramount importance to any organisation and must be carefully protected.

2: Data Disasters

What is meant by risk to data?

A risk to data is the potential for loss or corruption of that data. Every organisation depends on various kinds of simple, complex and historical data for running its day to day business. A simple piece of data can be the details of an organisation's customers input to an Excel® spreadsheet and stored on a computer's hard disk. A complex piece of data may be the details of millions of credit card transactions held in a huge software database inside a major organisation, such as, VISA or MasterCard.

Depending on the user, department or organisation, a loss or corruption of any of the pre-mentioned data can result in an array of business problems. Therefore, the protection and safe retrieval of data are of the utmost importance to any organisation.

Why and how do companies lose data?

Computer data is a virtual, rather than a physical item, and cannot be protected by security guards, guard dogs or insurance. Organisations often lose valuable data for a number of reasons - some of which are as follows:

- Many do not invest in sufficient costs and resources to perform regular system back-ups and install suitable anti-virus software, because they believe that if an old and used computer fails to function, it can simply be discarded in the same way as any other electrical appliance. However, what they fail to understand is that regular electrical appliances, for example, refrigerators and fans, do not hold data, whereas computers do. Therefore, if a computer should suddenly fail, an organisation will instantly lose its data, hence computers should not be treated in the same way as other electrical appliances.

- Some do not have suitable and appropriately qualified members of technical staff to maintain their computer systems.

- Lack of appropriate uninterrupted power supplies can also cause disk failures, resulting in loss of data.

- Data is stored haphazardly – on out-dated floppy disks, CD-ROMs, local hard disks, pen drives, USB sticks, etc. No processes are in place to clearly identify data storage locations to end-users.

- They may not budget for the cost of appropriate and adequate anti-virus software tools. A virus attack can wipe out years of data very quickly.

An organisation's business managers may think that in the event of a computer-related disaster, experienced members of its technical staff can simply be immediately replaced from some outsourcing, or external organisation. However this is no easy task, and could even be impossible. For example, it would be difficult for an external IT person; however qualified, to simply walk into an organisation and start assisting in DR, BC or data recovery. It often takes several weeks or months for an IT professional to gain a full understanding of the nature and function of IT in any organisation.

How should organisations store data safely?

An organisation should consider how to store and recover data as soon as a decision is taken to computerise its operations; regardless of whether it's for use by one person only, or a department. Data back-up strategies need to be developed in order to determine the timeframes, technologies, media and off-site storage of the back-ups. This will also ensure that a recovery point and time objectives can be met. Depending on the size of an organisation and its scale of operations, data storage can be one or more of the following:

- A small organisation may have only one or two computers. They may have a single directory, or folder, on the hard disk that is named 'data', where all of its data is created, saved and accessible – perhaps, for example, simply in the format of Word® and Excel® documents. As a DR measure, each day a user could copy all files to an alternative location, such as, a CD-ROM, or low capacity USB disk. Then, in the event of computer failure, or a disk crash, the operating system can be reloaded and the data directory copied and returned to its original location from the CD-ROM or USB disk.

- A small to medium sized organisation may have several computers, and opt to dedicate a larger one as a data storage server for all other users - usually called a file server. This allows users to create files, such as documents or spreadsheets on their local computers, but save and store them to specified locations on the file server. The file server could have a number of directories or folders named, for example, finance, design, HR, etc., that each department can use as storage for their important files. The file server could be attached with a small tape drive, or an external hard disk that will perform a daily system back-up of all the specified directories and folders on the server. In the event of a file server crash, or an accidental deletion of files, IT can restore the folders after the server has been fixed.

- A large organisation may have hundreds, or even thousands of computers and servers of all types, that could be in the format of file servers, database servers, web servers, e-mail servers, etc. Enterprise planning is required to ensure that users store their data on properly identified servers - each of which may be backed up using high capacity tape drives, archival systems, mirror servers, etc. Very large organisations, such as Ford, Shell and IBM will have hundreds of servers of various types containing terabytes of important data, which require large investments in back-up equipment and qualified members of staff. Depending on the time available or technical limitations, it can be a centralised back-up or a distributed backup.

What are some of the most common storage and back-up options?

There are various common storage and back-up options available, but there's no single solution for everyone. They may be in the form of an inexpensive pen drive, or USB, that's capable of storing a couple of gigabytes of memory, to expensive tape libraries and network filers that are able to store several terabytes of data. Extremely large tape libraries that can back up mainframes can easily cost in the region of six to seven figures. New, advanced technologies are available on back-up devices to dramatically improve back-up speeds, and are able to back up large amounts of data in a short period of time. Some of the common storage and back-up devices are as follows:

- DATs (Digital Audio Tapes), ranging from 2 to 24 gigabytes.

- DLTs (Digital Linear Tapes), from 20 to 80 gigabytes.

- SDLTs (Super Digital Linear Tapes), 40 to 100 gigabytes.

- LTOs (Linear Tape Open), 100 to 300 gigabytes.

- Tape Libraries of LTO or DLT. These can hold between seven to twenty tapes inside one box. Combined back-up capacities will exceed a terabyte or more.

- Special tape drives for bigger machines like large mainframes, AS/400s, UNIX boxes, etc.

The above devices usually come with their own back-up software, or are compatible with industry standard back-up software that is readily available on the market.

Methods of back-up: The following are some of the common methods of backing up data.

- **Standard:** Basic file back-up option.

- **Open files option:** Used to back up files even though some users could be accessing them.

- **Database back-up option:** Used to back up online databases.

- **E-mail back-up:** Used to back up e-mail servers.

- **Remote back-up:** Used to back up workstations, laptops, etc., that are connected to a network.

- **Image back-up:** Used to take a snapshot of the entire hard disk, sector by sector as a single image file. In the event of a disk crash the image file can be used to rebuild and restore the hard disk to its original condition on the same machine. It's also possible to restore the image file on an identical new hard disk on an identical machine model.

What is meant by Recovery Time Objective (RTO) and Recovery Point Objective (RPO)?

The terms RTO and RPO (referred to in *Chapter 15*), are often used in DR discussions to define the time and data tolerance that an organisation is willing to accept, usually in terms of loss of data and business downtime before it's able to recover and resume with business as usual.

RTO defines the time-scale (in hours or days) within which this must be achieved, that is, the length of time it can afford to cease operating its business. Therefore, if it's able to tolerate a timescale of one business day, then the RTO is one business day.

RPO defines the point in time when an organisation should recover, for example, it could be stated as '*Data can be recovered as of 9 pm last night*' - it defines the amount of data that it can afford to lose. If an organisation performed daily back-ups of a critical server at night, and the server was to fail the following afternoon, it will only be possible to restore data up to the point of the previous night. Therefore, the RPO will be defined as that of the previous day's close of business.

An organisation could prepare a table, such as *Table 4,* for all of its critical systems and tackle each one individually.

Table 4: RTO and RPO for critical systems

SYSTEM	RTO	RPO
Development server	One business day	Data restored as of previous business day.
Finance system	One day	Data restored as of previous business day.
Data connectivity	Four hours	N/A

Organisations must be able to resume their business operations quickly, and many would prefer this to be at the point from which its operations were disrupted or stopped, so that the last data entry or transaction is preserved. This would require the availability of 100% of the data on alternative systems 100% of the time, but these can be very expensive. The shorter the delay - the less data is lost, and the sooner the business can resume its operations. Therefore, if there is no tolerance for loss of data, an online back-up and archival system must be used. RTO and RPO must be decided in the specific context of a particular organisation.

What is Internet back-up?

Internet service providers also provide options for backing up important data to a server. This service makes it possible for a user to copy important data to a secure server or disk space dedicated to an organisation. A simple utility, or software, can be installed on a computer or server that allows the user to schedule back-ups, select files and folders to be backed-up, password protect files etc. Data can also be encrypted for transmission. Many organisations are currently reluctant to have their data stored using the Internet, but with the correct security practices established, it is becoming a more popular method of back-up. More information about internet based services (called Cloud services) is provided in the chapter on cyber security.

What is a 'geocluster'?

A 'geocluster' is an abbreviation for geographic cluster, which is a very expensive back-up option, and as such, may not be appropriate for a small or medium sized organisation. They are usually used by very large organisations that have a requirement to maintain international data synchronization. It's comprised of a number of servers that operate in tandem, thus providing load balancing and fail-over services. For example, if an organisation wants to keep a mirror of an important data server at an alternative location, for example a DR site in a different city or country, a 'geocluster' can be used to constantly keep the main and back-up server in synchronization.

How often should back-ups be taken, and what should be backed up?

Ideally, an organisation should carry out a back-up of all its data on a daily basis, although some may take a full back-up at the weekend and incremental back-ups daily. As an organisation becomes more dependent on computers and data for running its day-to-day business operations, storage and retrieval of data becomes of paramount importance. It should ensure that all important data is regularly backed-up and stored in appropriate fire and waterproof safe. It should also ensure that end-users only store their data on specified files, e-mail and database servers that are regularly backed-up. Therefore, in the event of any loss or accidental deletion of data, IT staff can restore the previous day's data to the user. Users should also be educated on the process to prevent the storage of any important data on local hard disks or pen drives that can't be recovered if damaged.

How can one decide what data needs to be backed-up?

The decision on the data that an organisation should back up should be taken using the input of each of its head of departments to ascertain the data that's considered to be of importance, and which it can't afford to lose. This should be followed with the provision of secure folders and other server accesses to the respective users, who should be educated on the process to ensure that important data is stored at the specified server locations only. These should be regularly backed up, and the back-ups should be periodically tested by restoring them on a test location.

Some organisations back up all of its data that is stored on a server, which in some instances could be a useful practice. However, it could also lead to time consuming back-ups and unnecessary memory storage consumption if users store non-business related files, such as songs or images. Therefore, users should ensure that only business related files are stored and not personal files.

How and where should back-up tapes be stored?

The location for storing data back-up tapes is of paramount importance. Back-up tapes can easily become damaged by heat and moisture so they must be stored in an appropriate and secure location. Some of the best practices for storing and using tapes are as follows:

- After every back-up, tapes should be labelled and stored in a fire and water-proof safe in a non-humid area.

- Back-up tapes should not be stored inside, or near the data centre. This is to ensure that the tapes don't get destroyed in the event of a disaster, for example, fire or flood.

- Data tapes are usually stored off-site at an alternative location to that of the organisation. Also, the same back-up tapes should not be used for a long period of time, because they have a tendency of losing their magnetic retention.

- Old tapes should be periodically tested for their ability to restore data, and if they fail the test any necessary precautions should be taken immediately, for example, taking a new back-up on a new tape.

- Old tapes should be destroyed safely and securely. Study and implement all the manufacturers' recommendations for the model of back-up tape and drive purchased.

How often should back-ups be tested?

The testing of backups is a very important exercise. An organisation's IT department could be backing-up data for a number of years, but have never had the opportunity to test whether or not the data can be retrieved from the tapes. Hence, it is necessary to test every back-up tape periodically to determine whether the data can be retrieved. If a server fails at the same time that a tape isn't readable, then this could be a disaster. It is highly advisable to plan a regular schedule for restoring a sizeable amount of data to a test location from each and every back-up tape. This will allow an end-user to verify whether the data restored to the test location is correct and readable. These exercises can be made part of an organisation's DR policy to prevent data recovery surprises.

Will taking proper data back-ups daily ensure DR?

Carrying out daily data back-ups alone is not enough to ensure DR. Back-ups, whether on tape, or other media, will simply ensure that the data is safe. DR is a different issue. Having only the data on a back-up tape will be of no use if the file server is destroyed. In order to have proper DR safeguards and recovery methods, and to prevent a disaster striking the servers in the first place, an organisation should invest in the following additional precautions:

- **Maintenance:** Comprehensive hardware maintenance contracts for all critical servers to ensure that any contractors repair, or replace, faulty equipment within the tolerated time scale.

- **Spares:** On-site availability of spare parts, for example, hard disks, power supplies, or even a spare machine.

- **Mirror servers:** Depending on low tolerable downtime, some organisations may even invest in having mirrored servers for mission critical functions

- **UPS:** Uninterrupted power supply to all critical equipment.

- **Fire prevention mechanisms:** The place where servers are housed should not be near any fire hazards, for example, a kitchen below the data centre.

- **Water seepage prevention:** The place where servers are housed should not have any major water sources, for example, an overhead tank above the ceiling.

- **Security:** Unauthorised access prevention.

- **Anti-virus:** Anti-virus prevention, with anti-virus updates.

- **Updates:** Applying proper service packs, hot fixes, basic input/output system updates, driver updates, etc., as recommended or supplied by the equipment or software manufacturer, and any other manufacturer's recommendations.

Some questions to ask before starting back-ups on critical servers and equipment:

- Is there a complete list of critical equipment that needs to be backed up daily? Has any important equipment been forgotten?

- Is it known what needs to be backed up in each of the above critical equipment?

- Who is assigned to take back-ups?

- How is the back-up taken?

- For what length of time should back-ups be stored?

- Who is authorized to initiate restores; if necessary?

- Will back-up tapes need to be stored off-site?

(For a few more Where, How, Why, When, and What questions: refer to *Chapter 15* 'Plenty of Questions').

What is 'disk mirroring'?

'Disk mirroring' is the duplication of data in real time across two separate hard disks within a single machine, or between two machines, thereby ensuring continuous availability and accuracy. If a server has two disks of identical capacity, it's possible to establish a mirror between them, so that the data on primary disk-1 always gets mirrored to secondary disk-2. Hence, if disk-1 fails, disk-2 will have all the data of primary disk-1 intact. Disk mirroring can be software-based or hardware-based, although hardware-based mirroring is superior. Third party software and hardware is available as a package, and has a number of useful and configurable features that aren't directly available with the basic operating system or hardware.

What is a 'database replication'?

An organisation may depend on specialised files called databases that are able to hold a variety of information in a single computer file. These databases can be accessed and updated by many people simultaneously. Some of the common names in databases are SQL, Oracle, DB2, and MS-Access. Corruption or deletion of a database file can wipe out data that's been entered over a number of years, and been accessed by a great many users. Therefore, it is vital that adequate precautions are taken when handling and maintaining databases. Specially-qualified members of staff and database administrators are required to manage them. A database replication is a partial or full duplication of data from a source database to a destination database. If, for example, a database server holds a database by the name of CUSTDATA (customer data), then replication can periodically pump all of that data into another database file named CUSTDATABKUP that's held on a different server. Replication may use any one of a number of methods – synchronous, asynchronous, and mirroring. So, if the main server fails, it is still possible to extract all data from the back-up database server. Special back-up tools are available that can be used to automatically replicate a main database's contents into another database. Various low to high-end database synchronization tools, with different features are available.

What does 'server load balancing' mean?

Many heavy-duty applications cannot run on one single machine alone. There could be many users accessing such an application, and as a result of this the server may get bogged down, unable to service the large number of simultaneous requests. This is where the server load balancing technique is necessary. It uses multiple servers to host a common application, thus allowing the automatic distribution of traffic across multiple servers running a common application, so that no one server is overloaded. A group of servers appears as a single server to the network. Server load balancing can be implemented among servers within a site or among servers on different sites. Using load balancing among different sites can enable the application to continue to operate as long as one or more sites remain operational.

How can one prevent loss of IT equipment?

IT equipment can be broadly classified into two categories:

- Equipment that holds organisation and user data, such as, file servers, database servers, hard disks, tapes, laptops, etc.

- Equipment that does *not* hold organisation or user data, such as LAN switches, hubs, routers, monitors, etc.

It is more important to protect equipment that holds data, than it is to protect equipment that doesn't. However, it does not mean the latter is of any less importance, but that an organisation's data is of a higher priority and of paramount importance to it. Equipment that holds data can't be purchased from external sources, whereas non-data equipment can be purchased off-the-shelf from several vendors and reconfigured. For example, if an important file server is damaged beyond repair, the situation cannot be resolved by simply purchasing a new one, because the lost data can't be purchased with it. On the other hand, if the same damage was to happen to a LAN switch that connects several machines together, a new replacement can be purchased immediately, and it can be reconfigured to its standard settings. Some of the specific precautions for critical equipment that holds data are as follows:

- Have standby power supplies, hard disks, or even spare machines if possible.

- Ensure that the equipment is under complete comprehensive warranty and insured.

- Ensure full, daily back-ups are completed. Insist and verify that all members of staff store important business related data only, on identified server locations that get backed up every day.

- Have all user manuals, CD-ROMs, bootable disks and repair disks to hand.

- Verify data integrity regularly by restoring data to a test location.

- Do not store all important data on a single server. Have multiple physical servers to split the load.

- Have ownership of useful recovery tools, such as Disk Repair, File Undelete, Registry Recover, etc. and become familiar with their usage.

Other standard methods to protect data are listed below.

On-site disaster prevention methods:

- System data should be fully backed up on a daily basis

- Data tapes and storage medium stored properly in fire- and water-proof safes

- Essential spares are available, for example, power supplies and spare hard disks Servers are under a comprehensive hardware maintenance guarantee by a qualified contractor, backed by a responsive service level agreement (SLA)

- Servers are housed in a secure data centre with clean, uninterrupted power supplies (UPS)

- Servers are maintained by qualified and trained members of staff

- Servers and data access is restricted to authorised members of staff only

- Servers are protected from viruses and hackers by anti-virus and intrusion detection systems

- Installation of all necessary upgrades, service packs, hot fixes, driver updates and bug fixes to prevent faults

- Clear step-by-step documents to assist in data restoration and replacement of spares

- Insurance to cover theft, fire and damage to equipment.

- Hot standby server in a DR or BC site, preferably identical to the one in the main site in all respects.

- Automatic or manual data synchronization between main and standby server.

- Copies of every important document, for example test plans placed in the DR or BC site.

- Testing and periodic dry runs at the DR or BC site.

- Other essential information and precautions suggested by the manufacturer for their equipment.

- Ensure that the technical support team is responsible for full and proper back-ups of all servers on a daily basis.

- Invest in good quality tape drives and other back-up devices.

- Ensure that all important data is stored only on servers that are backed up on a daily basis, and back up important information daily.

- Learn how to restore data properly.

- Store tapes and key papers in fire and water-proof safes.

- Test whether old back-up tapes can be read, and that data can be restored from them.

- Don't allow members of staff to store business data on their local drives.

- Don't allow unauthorised access to servers and databases.

- Don't allow data to exceed tape drive capacity.
- Don't use the same tapes for a long period of time.

CHAPTER 3: VIRUS DISASTERS

'Disasters normally don't come alone. They usually bring their family along.'

Anonymous

What is a computer virus?

A computer virus is a software program, that is usually written by an intelligent troublemaker (unethical software programmer), to wreak havoc on other computer programs. They may come in all shapes and forms and serve no useful purpose. The intention of a virus is to exploit any vulnerability in an operating system or program, and they have caused a substantial amount of financial damage to many organisations worldwide. Some viruses are harmless and can simply pop up with annoying messages, whereas others are deadly and can very quickly completely wipe out the data on a hard disk. A virus attack can happen very quickly, and users don't usually notice the damage until it is too late. Technically speaking, a virus is usually an executable file designed to replicate itself while avoiding detection. It may disguise itself as a legitimate program, and they are often rewritten to avoid detection. Hence, anti-virus programs must be continuously updated to detect new and modified viruses. Viruses are the number one method of computer vandalism.

How can an organisation protect itself from viruses?

In order for an organisation to protect its computers from virus attacks, each and every computer must have anti-virus software installed that is regularly updated. Several reputable manufacturers exist who can provide excellent virus prevention and cleaning tools for desktops, laptops, tablets, and even large server systems. The number of viruses that lurk around the Internet are too numerous to count, and it isn't enough to simply install an anti-virus program in the hope that it will provide protection from every type of virus. An anti-virus program must be periodically updated to protect a computer from the latest viruses. Some of the best practices to prevent viruses are as follows:

- Install a reputable anti-virus program on all computers, that is, desktops, laptops, tablets and servers.

- Update new virus definitions periodically, or as and when the manufacturer provides an update.

- Scan all machines periodically.

- Prevent users from downloading and installing free software programs and files from the Internet.

- Install URL filters. These are programs that prevent users from accessing unwanted or unauthorised websites.

- Prevent users from accessing personal e-mail, such as, Yahoo!, Hotmail and Gmail from within the organisation, because they could receive viruses via attachments sent by unknown persons.

- Scan every incoming and outgoing e-mail. Educate or prevent users from using removable storage devices between the home and office, because a home computer could easily be infected with a virus that could spread through a pen drive brought into the office.

- Install proper service packs, hot fixes and program updates for the operating system and other applications to fix vulnerabilities that could be exploited by viruses.

- Prevent members of staff from using personal internet connections on office systems via data cards. Ensure that all internet access is via proper firewalls.

- Install internet firewalls with virus detectors.

- Educate users about new viruses and their symptoms.

What is a worm?

Worms are very similar to viruses in that they are computer programs that replicate copies of themselves (usually to other computer systems via network connections), and wreak havoc on a large number of computers within a short period of time. Worms aren't like regular file viruses that attach themselves to other files or programs - they exist as separate entities, but because of their similarity they are often referred to as a virus. A well-known example of a worm is the 'ILOVEYOU' worm, which invaded millions of computers through e-mail in 2000. A more recent example of a dangerous virus that infected millions of computers was the Conficker virus in 2008, which blocked access to all antivirus manufacturer sites.

What is a Trojan?

A Trojan is named after the wooden horse that was used by the Greeks to infiltrate Troy. It's a program that performs an undocumented action; as intended by the programmer, but one that the user wouldn't approve of if they were aware of it.

What is a macro-virus?

A macro is a piece of code that can be embedded in a data file. Some word processing software, for example, Microsoft® Word® and spreadsheet programs, such as, Microsoft® Excel®, allow the attachment of macros to the documents they create. This enables documents to control and customise the behaviour of the programs that created them, or even extend the capabilities of the program.

In many respects, macro-viruses are the same as all other viruses, except they are attached to data files, as opposed to executable programs. Any application which supports document macros that automatically execute is a ripe target for macro-viruses. An example of a macro-virus is the Melissa virus. It's delivered via e-mail as a Word® document attachment with the filename List.doc.

In addition, there are a number of other types of viruses, and an organisation will have to ensure that it's protected from them all.

How can an organisation recover after a virus attack?

In spite of the precautions an organisation may have taken, it remains susceptible to a virus attack if there are any loopholes. In the event of an attack, IT support should immediately initiate emergency measures. Some of the common actions to take in response to an attack are as follows:

- Immediately disconnect and isolate the infected machine from the network.

- Switch off internet access.

- Run an anti-virus scan and try to remove the virus using various tools and updates.

- Reformat the machine if necessary.

- In extreme cases, rebuild or restore the last known good back-up.

- Switch off other machines on the network to prevent the virus spreading.

- Seek the advice of an anti-virus contractor and take any recommended action to remove the virus.

- Only after it has been determined that the virus has been destroyed, should any machines be reconnected to the network.

Important warning: Never try to test an anti-virus program by releasing a live virus into an organisation.

Note: It is not always possible to recover from a virus attack. Data of great financial value has been lost worldwide, because of non-recoverable virus attacks. Although it may be possible to eventually find a cure for a new and dangerous type of virus, by this time the damage will usually have been done. Therefore, the best method of prevention is to take all necessary and continuous precautions.

How does one update anti-virus software on all machines?

It is vital to ensure that the latest anti-virus program and its updates protect every machine that an organisation uses. This is can actually be a Herculean task, depending on the size of an organisation and its nature of business. In a smaller organisation that has few computers, its members of IT support staff can manually update anti-virus software on all machines. However, for a larger organisation that has a larger number of machines, it may not be possible to update the anti-virus software on each machine, on a regular basis. It is necessary to use one or more of the following methods:

- Update anti-virus software when machines logon to the main server or domain through login scripts, or by installing anti-virus deployment servers.

- Enable automatic updates on all machines to connect to a server that holds updates, and install them automatically through specialised scripts or batch files.

- Install an anti-virus deployment server that will automatically scan all machines on the network, and deploy updates automatically at specified intervals.

- Ensure all members of field staff update anti-virus software on their laptops by sending periodic reminders and methods to update.

- Implement all of the manufacturer's recommendations.

3: Virus Disasters

Dos and don'ts regarding viruses

Do

- Purchase a reputable anti-virus program and have sufficient licences to cover all computers, laptops and servers.

- Make it mandatory to update every computer with the latest patches and virus fixes.

- Password-protect the anti-virus program, so that ordinary users are unable to disable or uninstall the program.

- Educate users on how to prevent viruses getting into their computers.

- Scan every data device brought into an organisation by visitors

- Check every incoming and outgoing e-mail for viruses using automated tools.

Don't

- Allow members of staff to bring in personal removable storage devices.

- Allow members of staff to download games, screen savers, utilities or shareware from the Internet.

- Test any live, old or new, viruses on the network as a means of testing whether the anti-virus program is able to detect and catch it.

What is 'phishing'?

Phishing is a major threat to many organisations that conduct business via the Internet, and customers that purchase goods by credit card or operate an online bank account. A fraudster may falsely claim to be a legitimate bank or organisation, and send an e-mail to a user in an attempt to scam them into providing private information that can be used for identity theft. 'Spoofed' e-mails lead consumers to counterfeit websites designed to trick recipients into divulging financial data, such as, credit card numbers, account usernames, passwords and answers to security questions. For example, a hoax e-mail will ask for a customer's bank account and login details under the pretext that there's a problem with their user ID, or because the bank is updating their information. Following this, the e-mail directs the unsuspecting user to visit an authentic-looking, but bogus website where they are asked to update their personal information to that held by the legitimate organisation. It's possible that a bogus website can be created that looks exactly the same as that of a legitimate bank's website. If a user was to provide their account details, this would allow a fraudster to withdraw or transfer money into their accounts and it may never be known until it's too late. This is a financial disaster to the user, and the legitimate organisation may suffer damage to its reputation, become involved in legal battles, and face insurance claims.

What about safety on mobile devices?

With the advent of hand held devices, such as tablets and smartphones, more and more people are using such devices as a means of communication and making bank transactions. Such devices have now become the target of troublemakers, by the release of malware and the use of remote data readers, key loggers, etc. Therefore, it's highly recommended that a suitable anti-virus is installed on all mobile devices, because viruses are no longer only computer related.

CHAPTER 4: COMMUNICATION SYSTEM DISASTERS

'I beg you take courage; the brave soul can mend even disaster.'
Catherine the Great (1729-96)

What are some of the common methods of communication in organisations?

Organisations have come a long way in exchanging information internally and externally from the good old days of plain telephones and telex. Today we have a variety of voice and data communication methods that companies have become heavily accustomed to. In fact, many would practically shut down if their communication links fail. For example, a large, well established online book seller like Amazon.com may lose hundreds of thousands of pounds if communication links to their website fail for even a short period of time, say during a peak shopping time like Christmas. Even a smaller organisation or contractor will suffer if its communication systems fail beyond an acceptable limit.

What is a communication failure?

Before the popularity of, and dependence on, the Internet, many organisations worked as isolated silos. The main method of communication with the outside world was by means of telephones, telex, or facsimile, whereas today an organisation has a number of methods, and is extremely dependent on them, for example:

- Local Area Network within an office

- Campus networks

- Wide Area Networks between its offices

- E-mail (internal and external)

- Private data leased lines connecting its various branch offices within a city, country or worldwide

- Private voice leased lines connecting its various branch offices within a city, country or worldwide

- Virtual private networks via the Internet connecting its branches or external suppliers, consultants and telecommuters.

- Wireless communication.

These services are usually provided by external contractors and service providers, and an organisation may be directly and indirectly dependent on such external sources for its business communication requirements. Failures in communication can occur at any time, and a disconnection or problem in any of the above communication modes can disable an organisation's business functions. Each and every method of communication is prone to risks and outages. For example, if it depends on e-mail to provide support functions to its customers, and the system is down, then it will be unable to provide this service. Hence, an organisation must ensure that it has more than one method of communication should the primary method fail for all their critical functions.

Some of the common communication DR methods or workable alternatives are listed below:

- If the Local Area Network fails, it's possible to have standby switching equipment that provides essential services to end-users.

- If connection to its branch offices is via a private leased line, it can also implement a slow speed dial-up line in parallel, or have multiple leased lines that can be used if the main one fails.

- If connection to the Internet via a dedicated line is lost, it can have a few standalone internet stations via dial-up.

- If a private voice network is down it can use paid services, such as international direct dialling (IDD).

- Telephone services from more than one service provider to avoid failure in one or the other.

- More than one method of standard communication, for example, customer support can be provided via e-mail, telephone, facsimile, or by logging on to a website and posting a message.

What are some of the methods for preventing Local Area Network failures?

A Local Area Network (LAN) is an important method of connecting computers within an organisation. It's no longer possible to use only standalone computers to store or access data. All must be linked in order to send and receive data, and have access to the Internet and e-mail. They are linked using high-end equipment, such as switches and hubs. A high quality switch box has ports that are able to connect any number of computers – from one or two, to hundreds.

Some common methods of preventing LAN disasters are as follows:

- **Physical redundancy:** Have multiple switches for connecting computers. These are available with a range of 8 to 48 ports, but if cascaded, can provide even more. Therefore, it is better to purchase a number of 24-port or 48-port switches and cascade them, as opposed to one integrated switch that has 200 ports. This will ensure that if any switch fails it will affect only a small number of users.

- **Standby equipment:** Sufficient standby equipment should be available for critical equipment. For example, a spare switch to connect servers and other critical equipment should the main switch fail.

- **Maintenance contract:** Ensure that switches are under proper and comprehensive maintenance from reputable contractors for speedy replacement during failures. If an organisation has little or no time tolerance, ensure its IT department has critical spares on-site.

- **Updating patches:** Install all manufacturers recommended patches, firmware upgrades, etc., periodically. Such upgrades fix many design faults in the systems.

- **Proper UPS:** Keep all switches powered by clean UPS and housed in dust-free cool locations.

What are some methods for preventing WAN disasters?

In today's distributed environment, losing Wide Area Network (WAN) connectivity can disable an organisation's ability to function just as effectively as a massive data centre outage. Here are some best practices for designing and developing a resilient WAN:

- **Physical redundancy:** Make sure there are separate cables to provide separate services. For example, if there is one long distance service provider that provides three WAN links, have them all on separate physical cables running on different paths. Label every link properly to speedily troubleshoot in the event of a link failure.

- **Physical risk:** Ensure each link is secure from water seepages, accidental cuts due to digging, thefts, etc.

- **Routing redundancy:** This is a logical redundancy. For example, if the main WAN link between office 1 and office 2 fails, configure the network so that the data can be routed via office 3. This is called logical switching and is possible with transmission control internet protocol (TCIP) networks.

- **Multiple service providers:** If possible, purchase WAN links from more than one service provider.

- **Service provider DR plan:** Ensure that the WAN service provider has a demonstrable DR plan.

- **Dial-up lines:** Have an integrated services digital network (ISDN) back up dial-up link connecting all offices to be used in the event of a major WAN crisis. Test the dial-up links periodically.

- **Voice connectivity:** Ensure there are multiple modes of voice connectivity, for example mobile phones and land-line telephones, IP telephones, internet telephony, and even older methods of communication, such as, facsimiles and telex. Don't decommission any mode of communication fully, even if it's outdated – keep a small working set up for emergency purposes. One never knows when they may be of use.

- **External consultancy:** Have the WAN tested and certified by reputable external consultants.

Dos and don'ts regarding communication systems

Do

- Have more than one mode of communication for every business unit. Implement direct telephone lines, mobile phones and e-mail access for all necessary areas.

- Select communication systems and services from a number of different service providers as opposed to one provider, so that in the event of a system service failure by one provider, there is an alternative available.

- Ensure communication links, cables, connections, etc., are secure and tamper-proof.

Don't

- Purchase all communication services from a single service provider.

- Buy more band-width than is normally required.

CHAPTER 5: SOFTWARE DISASTERS

'The inhabitants of every civilized country are menaced; all desire to be saved from impending disaster; the overwhelming majority refuses to change their habits of thought, feeling and action which are directly responsible for their present plight.'

Aldous Huxley

What is a software disaster?

For an organisation to function, it will need several different types of computer. Each computer usually has pre-installed software known as the operating system, for example, Windows® 7, Windows® 8, or Linux. However, with only the operating system installed it isn't possible to do anything useful. Additional software known as an application, such as, Microsoft® Office®, databases, e-mail, web software, finance applications, reporting tools and business applications also have to be installed for them to be of use in a work environment.

Such software is normally provided by third-party contractors, or is sometimes developed in-house. It's very complicated, and can fail in a number of ways, some of which may be minor, and some major. For example, organisations usually use popular databases, such as SQL or Oracle, but if the complete database is corrupted due to a power problem or a virus, the organisation can be out of action for a number of days, or even weeks. Viruses can also destroy the data in a number of ways, and this can be classified as a software disaster.

What is a mission critical application?

A mission critical application is any software application that is essential to the organisation to perform its key business functions. For example, a software application that manages the deposit and withdrawal of bank funds can be classified as a mission critical application, that is, a bank won't be able to operate without it. Similarly, an application can also be classified as mission critical depending on the importance of it. The loss or stoppage of a mission critical application may have a negative impact on the organisation, together with possible legal or regulatory repercussions. For example, if an organisation, such as VISA or MasterCard, was to lose its critical credit card transactions system, it would have a significant impact in terms of revenue, reputation, legal issues and other problems. Therefore, it's vital to take care of any mission critical applications with the utmost care, and ensure that data is adequately protected and available at all times.

What are some of the software disasters that can strike an organisation?

An organisation must ensure that every item of software it uses is fully tested under various conditions before they deploy it in the 'production environment'. The selection of software for each department must also be carried out carefully. In addition, a proper change management procedure is necessary to ensure a smooth upgrade (with roll-back options) for every new software change.

Some of the common types of software disaster are as follows.

Operating system related

Operating systems, such as, Windows®, Linux® and UNIX® are used on many computers worldwide, and although the manufacturers take every precaution to provide a stable product, they can't ensure it will never fail. Operating systems are so complex that there are always loopholes and vulnerabilities that can be exploited by viruses and other programs. There may also be design faults that need to be fixed over time. For example, Microsoft® has released a number of operating systems, but has since released several hot fixes and service packs that must be applied to eliminate bugs and defects, thus making the product more stable and trouble-free. An organisation should ensure it uses the latest version of an operating system, and periodically applies any service patches and bug fixes supplied by the manufacturer, as problems are discovered. Furthermore, if using these operating systems it must ensure that every machine is updated with the latest patches to protect them from design faults. However, the installation of updates must first be fully tested in order to verify that it won't cause problems with any other applications. For example, if a file server running an operating system with Service Pack 1 was supporting an important finance application, and suddenly the machine was upgraded with Service Pack 2; without testing, there may be a software conflict which causes the application to stop working. This could be classified as a disaster, because it may not be possible to revert to the server's original state easily, or speedily. However, if the update was tested on a test machine that replicates the production environment before it was applied, the crisis could have been avoided.

Application-related

Similar to an operating system, there are various types and versions of other software packages, for example e-mail, databases, reporting, development, testing, monitoring and business applications. Each of these can have a number of updates and patches supplied by the respective manufacturer as a fix for different bugs and design faults that have been identified - all which must also be applied to ensure the smooth running of an application. However, proper care must be taken before updating patches and versions on an organisation's live servers.

Hardware-related

A particular item of software or operating system can misbehave if there are hardware design faults in the computer being used. Such faults can only be rectified by the hardware manufacturer, and are usually fixed by providing bios (basic input/output system), firmware, or driver updates. For example, an ill-mannered SCSI (small computer system interface - pronounced '*scuzzy*') disk driver can corrupt the data being stored on the hard disk SCSI, hence, the disk driver or the SCSI card firmware may need to be upgraded to rectify the error.

The IT support department should periodically check the supplier's websites of the associated products they use for any necessary updates, with the aim of installing them as soon as possible.

What are some of the best practices for software disaster prevention?

In view of the myriad of software programs and tools available, it's essential to manage software implementations properly. Some of the best practices to prevent common software disasters within an organisation are as follows:

- Ensure that every computer runs a single, common operating system, office applications and other software tools as far as possible. This will make support and troubleshooting easier. However, if a software bug, virus or hacker gains access to the network a large amount of damage can be inflicted within a short space of time. Therefore, a balanced approach is required to ensure alternative methods are available for each essential function.

- Ensure that every computer runs the same version of hot fixes and service packs. If any problems are noticed they will be visible on all machines and can be fixed once, permanently.

- Ensure that every computer is running the latest version of a reputable anti-virus program. Have a periodic and mandatory update policy to tackle new viruses.

- Do not apply service packs, hot fixes, upgrades, etc., without testing them first.

- Never interfere with software settings and features without understanding the consequences.

- Do not allow end-users to install any application or tools they wish.

- Do not allow end-users to download applications, free or shareware from the Internet.

- Do not allow end-users to download attachments from personal e-mail.

- Have a proper virus-scanning schedule for every server, desktop or laptop.

- Install manufacturer recommended bios, updates and driver updates for the computer. For example, video driver updates, disk driver updates, network card driver updates and bios updates for the motherboard. These updates usually fix various design flaws, or potential bugs and faults discovered by the manufacturer.

- Don't install more than one application or patch at the same time. For example, if a machine has to be updated with Windows® Service Pack 4, and an SQL Service Pack 3, then install each on a different day to see how the machine behaves - unless both need to be installed in a specific sequence to resolve an identified issue.

- Always take a complete back-up of necessary data and files before installing any new upgrades or patches.

- Always follow the manufacturer's steps for installation. Don't try to skip any steps or files unless the consequences are known.

- Accept the advice of professionals and contractors if unsure about an installation, because there could be several post-installation settings and configurations.

- A software development organisation should ensure that the source code and other applications developed by its programmers are stored or duplicated in more than one location, perhaps many times a day.

- Implement industry best practices and manufacturer recommendations.

- Don't use old and outdated software. Keep upgrading to the latest versions wherever possible.

CHAPTER 6: DATA CENTRE DISASTERS

'WHANGDEPOOTENAWAH, In the Ojibwa tongue, disaster; an unexpected affliction that strikes hard.'

Ambrose Bierce (1842-1914)

What is a data centre?

A computer data centre is a secure room, or rooms, where an organisation's mission critical servers and other important equipment are housed. A data centre is the heart of any modern organisation, and a disaster here can very quickly bring it to a complete standstill. Special precautions need to be taken to prevent IT disasters, especially within a data centre.

Example: Disaster inside a data centre

Building Security: "Hello Sir, this is the Building Security Officer calling. Sorry to wake you up in the middle of the night, but there was a fire in the office just now."

CIO: "Heavens. What was the damage?"

Building Security: "Not much, I think. Luckily the fire engine came within 20 minutes and doused out the fire. The fireman said the fire had damaged only a couple of computers. It didn't spread to other areas."

CIO: "That's a relief, any idea which computers they were?"

Building Security: "Only those two big black computers in the data centre - the ones with blinking green lights labelled Mainframe 1 and 2. They're burnt to a crisp, along with the cassettes that were stored behind them."

CIO: "Mainframe 1 and 2 and our backup tapes? Help"

How should a data centre be built?

A data centre should be built with extreme care and conform to all international safety standards. It should be located in a room that's spacious, fire and waterproof, anti-static, ventilated, air conditioned and has UPS. An organisation should ensure that suitably qualified professionals conform to all industry standards while carrying out work on the electrical and networking cables inside a data centre. It should also have proper security and access control facilities, so that no unauthorised person can enter the centre.

What are some of the best practices to prevent disasters inside data centres?

Several best practices exist to prevent disasters occurring inside data centres, so it isn't necessary to reinvent the wheel. Organisations exist that specialise in providing consultancy and implementation for building world class data centres. However, below is a list of some common best practices to prevent a disaster in a data centre:

- Ensure that it's fireproof and doesn't contain any flammable material, or have any near it. Any areas that may be beneath or above it should also be fire and waterproof.

6: Data Centre Disasters

- Install appropriate fire alarms, smoke detectors and fire extinguishers, and ensure they're in working condition.

- Ensure all critical equipment has UPS capable of withstanding long durations of mains power failure, and provide good quality back-up generators.

- Have only important servers and equipment inside.

- Have an external consultant, or fire department to periodically inspect and certify the premises.

- Ensure there's no water leakage or humidity anywhere nearby, and that it's not directly above or below any hazardous areas, for example a kitchen, or a place where fuel is stored.

- Don't allow unauthorised entry, or persons to operate any of its equipment.

- Have appropriate air conditioning to cool the IT equipment.

- Don't have any plants or other decorative material inside.

- Have static eliminators installed at key locations that will prevent electrostatic charges from gathering around carpets, doorknobs, etc. Static electricity is very dangerous, and can cause minor to major shocks to anybody touching a charged object. It can also cause electronic equipment to fail.

- Don't draw more power than recommended from any power supply outlet. Have proper fuses and circuit breakers installed.

- Ensure the data centre is free from pests.

- If lifting or relocating equipment, ensure that it's carried out by qualified personnel with the use of proper equipment.

- Don't stack equipment without installing it in proper racks. Ensure adequate ventilation and space for easy maintenance.

- Don't allow anyone to bring drinks or food inside, or touch any IT equipment with wet hands. Don't touch the motherboard or other electronic components when the chassis is opened for any reason.

- Always use high quality electrical and computer cables — even if there are less expensive, lower quality alternatives available.

- Store all manuals, original disks, CD-ROMs and licence numbers in a safe, documented, fireproof place. Keep multiple copies of every important document and an additional copy in the DR centre.

Other precautions to prevent IT disasters

- Always purchase branded and reputable hardware models, even though they may be slightly more expensive. Branded and reputable manufacturers invest in the necessary research and development to ensure that their products are tested and are fully supported, and that any upgrades and bug fixes are available to solve any problems. Unbranded and assembled computers can be a mixture of several unknown vendor products, and may be prone to problems that aren't supported by the supplier, For example, it may have a motherboard from one manufacturer and a video card from another. Therefore, in the event of a system problem, no one will take responsibility for it, or assist in resolving the issue.

- Ensure that members of technical staff undergo periodic training in the latest areas of IT support.

- Periodically replace servers, computers and software with the latest systems. Many manufacturers declare certain models and versions obsolete within two or three years and stop supporting them. If an organisation is using an out of date system or software, it's at risk of having no support if it fails.

- Ensure that server passwords are regularly changed and used only by authorised personnel. A critical server's password with an unauthorised or incompetent person is a disaster waiting to happen.

- Delete all unwanted user IDs periodically to prevent unauthorised use.

- Don't remove the chassis cover on any equipment before it's powered down. Attach a static discharge belt for additional safety. Some high-end servers allow hot pluggable hard disks that allow a hard disk to be installed when the system is running. Unless it's absolutely necessary to keep the system powered on, don't attempt to use such features, but power them down before carrying out an upgrade or repair.

- Periodically reduce the number of unwanted and old IT machines throughout the organisation.

- Always purchase tested and proven versions of software and hardware. If a manufacturer releases a new version of an operating system or office application, don't try to install it on all equipment immediately, simply to be ahead of the rest. Any new versions of software should be given time to stabilise in the market and then implement in a staged manner. It should be remembered that most software and operating system upgrades are one-way processes and cannot be easily reverted. For example, if it's decided to upgrade to the latest operating system, and it's later discovered that the critical finance applications don't function properly, then this could lead to a serious crisis.

CHAPTER 7: IT STAFF MEMBER DISASTERS

'There are men in the world who derive exaltation from the proximity of disaster and ruin, as others from success.'

Winston Churchill (1874-1965)

Who is meant by members of IT staff?

Every organisation will usually have several members of staff, or departments (internal or outsourced) for maintaining and troubleshooting the IT infrastructure. They are usually referred to as members of IT staff, technical support or technical assistance, and usually have specialised training and the necessary skills for maintaining critical IT equipment. For example, there may be a specialised team solely to manage back-ups and restorations of various servers, who are trained in using the software, that is, how and what to back up, how to restore, etc., or a dedicated team to manage and operate e-mail systems.

What are the general precautions to prevent disasters relating to members of IT staff?

No organisation can run its business without a proper and qualified IT department. Its members of staff are usually categorised as key or critical staff, because they handle the organisation's critical IT equipment. A people-related disaster such as a resignation, injury or death to one or more of its critical members of staff could easily paralyse an organisation. Ironically, it's possible to replace an organisation's Chief Executive Officer (CEO) overnight, but it's nearly impossible, or highly risky to suddenly replace key members of IT staff.

Common precautions to prevent IT staff related disasters in an organisation are:

- Don't locate all members of staff in one place, working at the same location, or in the same building. If something happened to that building, all critical staff could be affected, and this could have serious implications on getting the network up and running again.

- Ensure every member of staff is adequately trained in all, or most support services. It would be a risk having only one person who is able to operate the back-up software, or holds the administration passwords for all servers. If that person resigns, or has an accident, then no one else is able to take system back-ups, or perform administration activities.

- An employee's salary should meet, or better the industry standards, because good competitive salaries help ensure low rates of resignation and attrition.

- Have an adequate member of staff ratio: *see below.*

- Don't hire temporary members of staff simply to reduce costs, because they don't usually have commitment or loyalty, and will always be looking for better opportunities elsewhere. Furthermore, they may leave at any time at very short notice, resulting in serious IT service issues, and an improper and inadequate handover between service providers.

- When outsourcing for members of staff, ensure, and demand that they have the appropriate qualifications and experience.

What is an appropriate IT member of staff ratio?

In order for an organisation to maintain a large IT infrastructure, it's necessary to have a sufficient number of IT staff members to properly manage its various systems. Irrespective of the amount of automation, it still requires a sufficient number of qualified staff that can understand, control, manage and run the operations. However, many organisations fail to understand the importance of this issue, and try to maintain a large IT infrastructure with the bare minimum number of staff. Some common reasons for this could be to save on costs, or that it's unable, or unwilling to invest in more headcount. Managing a large IT infrastructure will put enormous pressure, stress and overheads on members of IT staff if the department is under-resourced. Most IT staff struggle to meet service expectations that are too high for the current sizes of their respective departments. This can result in frequent resignations, improper process compliance, delay in support, and other issues that will slowly engulf the organisation. The revenue loss due to an overloaded, under-staffed IT service team could be significantly higher than the saving in salaries of having twice the number of members of staff.

It isn't enough for an organisation to believe that they've implemented IT best practice, simply by preparing a few process documents, procedures and policies – they also need the right number of members of IT staff to put it into practice in the way it's recommended. Furthermore, there is no point in committing high levels of availability everywhere when there is a shortage of staff to maintain even basic services. This is where IT staff ratio will help.

An appropriate IT staff ratio means having the right number of staff for a certain number of end-users and IT equipment. For example, a general rule of thumb is to have a ratio of two members of IT staff to support 100 end-users that are using 100 computers, and about three or four servers. However, it would be unreasonable to have the same two IT staff continue to support the organisation when the strength grows to 200 end-users. Naturally, the number of staff will have to increase in direct proportion to the number of end-users. Many of an organisation's business managers may argue that it's possible to simply implement a few fancy tools and not increase its number of staff. However, in reality, such arguments usually don't work. Furthermore, tools that are able to replace a human being are usually very expensive, and will need highly-qualified members of staff to operate and maintain them - plus there will be ongoing costs. Hence, it's absolutely necessary for an organisation to ensure that it has the correct strength in numbers of staff, to maintain the expected levels of availability.

There's no magic number for the IT staff member ratio. An organisation will have to gather the following statistics and arrive at an optimum number:

- average number of end-user calls per day
- average number of call backlogs per day
- call response time compared to committed time
- user downtime
- user downtime calculated in financial terms

- growth of end-user count.

Organisations that wish to compete based on properly fulfilling commitments made to their external and internal customers must invest in the correct IT staff to end-user ratios in order to remain competitive.

What are the usual reasons for members of IT staff disasters?

Many organisations may have implemented computers, software and telecommunications for running their businesses. However, these are often undertaken without proper planning of any sort. Some of the common issues faced by organisations regarding its IT staff include:

- Roles and responsibilities are not clearly defined or non-existent.

- A single member or very small team of IT staff are responsible for anything and everything related to IT.

- Lack of clearly defined and simple processes.

- No service level agreements, contractor agreements, or technical training.

- Business and technical members of staff not in agreement. Poor management buy-in, inadequate funding, culture issues, resistance to change.

- No understanding of the essential factors of using IT, for example, having appropriate IT staff, exponential hardware and software budgets, on-going costs and frequent and mandatory upgrades.

- Members of technical staff concentrating on technical matters only, and unable, or unwilling, to understand business needs.

- No structured customer support mechanism, help desk or service desk facilities.

- No proactive IT trouble prevention methods, only reactive support. Problems get solved after they occur with no prevention mechanism in place.

- Members of staff using outdated tools and equipment, resulting in the IT department being out of sync with modern business demands.

What are some of the best practices to be followed by members of IT staff?

A proper IT service is a very important aspect of any IT department, but many organisations don't have appropriate processes in place to manage these services. Different organisations follow their own methods to provide internal IT support, but there are industry standard practices readily available that can be easily adopted by any organisation of any size. One of the best known is the Information Technology Infrastructure Library (ITIL®), which was created by the United Kingdom's Office of Government Commerce (OGC) and defines best practices for IT service management.

What are the main benefits of using ITIL?

Many organisations believe they have already implemented excellent IT services and don't need any change. This may be true, but only closer examination will establish whether it is possible that they are missing out on various processes that could enhance their IT department. The benefits of using ITIL in an organisation are vast.

- Proven and tested processes. No need to re-invent the wheel for implementing its IT services. Covers end-to-end.

- Improved quality of IT service for business functions.

- Reduced downtime, reduced costs, improved customer and end-user satisfaction.

- Measurable, controllable, recoverable.

- Proactive rather than reactive. Clearly defined roles, responsibilities, and activities.

- Greater understanding of IT and its limitations by the organisation. Its business will understand IT better.

- Continuous improvement, stability, and problem prevention.

- Improved image. Organisations will also learn what to commit, and what not to commit to their external customers.

- When organisations implement ITIL, DR and BC will become easier because the necessary precautions and best practices for IT support will gradually become a day to day activity.

How can change management prevent disasters?

If an appropriate change management procedure is adopted for all of an organisation's IT implementations, upgrades and maintenance, a number of foreseeable disasters can be prevented – and this has been meticulously implemented by many. Change management means that any changes must go through a series of approvals and sign-offs before they can be implemented. For example, the management shouldn't allow any unauthorised technical changes, such as additions, deletions, modifications, or replacements to any part of the IT infrastructure. A knowledgeable change management team will need to study the request for change, and assess it from several technical and non-technical angles before authorising it. Having a proper change management procedure in place can prevent several types of disaster, for example:

- Preventing any IT or network changes during critical periods. For example, an organisation that sells consumer goods over the Internet or through retail stores shouldn't disturb its IT infrastructure (on which they depend for sales) in any way during the Christmas period. What would happen if its members of IT staff installed an untested software patch just before Christmas on an organisation's online sales web server? If the patch misbehaves and the server crashes due to a virus, then the customers can't purchase the products during such a critical time, causing loss of revenue and reputational damage.

- An organisation shouldn't allow any maintenance activities (except emergency fixes) on production systems during business hours. This can help prevent any unexpected disasters and business disruptions. For example, if IT staff upgrade a software patch or anti-virus software on an office e-mail server during office hours and it misbehaves, the e-mail server can become inaccessible to all users. Instead, if the patch is applied after office hours, or first tested on a test server, then IT staff can take the necessary precautions to recover the server without creating chaos.

- All IT changes must, and should, have a proper back out plan. For example, if some software is to be upgraded on an important server, an accurate snapshot or baseline must be taken before it's installed, so if the upgrade should fail or cause some other unexpected problem, the system can be reverted back to the previous baseline. Specialised image back-up tools can help create accurate images or snapshots of the systems being upgraded or modified.

What are the other risks relating to members of IT staff?

Risks and disasters can be caused by every member of staff. However, risks from members of IT staff can be more severe, because they are specialised staff who may have complete access to all critical equipment. They may have access to equipment and data that even the CEO doesn't have. Of course, most organisations wouldn't be able to survive without having some IT staff, but care can be taken to minimise the risks relating to them.

- A disgruntled member of IT staff can be an enormous threat to an organisation. He or she can simply destroy data from critical equipment for revenge.

- Dissatisfaction among members of IT staff resulting from lack of growth opportunities, inadequate salaries and overworked/underpaid situations are all potential threats to an organisation.

- An inadequate IT staff ratio is also a potential risk, and a disaster waiting to happen. Not having enough members of staff can have a gradual reduction on an organisation's capability to be competitive. Problems will get fixed slowly, processes will not be followed, IT shortcuts become common-place, and data back-ups may not be regular. All of these can lead to disaster sooner or later.

- IT service is a serious business and should be handled by mature and responsible members of staff who have several years of proven experience.

- Resignation of critical members of IT staff: In this competitive world, qualified and experienced members of IT staff are always in high demand. An organisation should ensure that it retains its qualified staff as far as possible, and also have a sufficient number to be able to cope with unexpected resignations or 'poaching' by competitors.

CHAPTER 8: IT CONTRACTOR DISASTERS

'What you spend years building, someone or something could destroy overnight. Build anyway.'

Mother Theresa

Who is an IT contractor?

Any external organisation that supplies technology related equipment, software or services to an organisation is called an IT contractor. All organisations depend on a number of external and third-party agencies for hardware, software, telecom, support, consumables, spares and other IT equipment. This is because it isn't possible to run any organisation independently without depending on one or more IT contractors for supporting some critical equipment or function. Selecting the right contractor is, therefore, of utmost importance to ensure timely support and assistance during all problems.

What is an IT contractor-related disaster?

A disaster occurring to a critical IT contractor is indirectly a disaster for any organisation using their products. Assume an organisation has purchased a database application from a vendor to load all its critical financial and other information. If the vendor goes bankrupt as a result of some internal disaster, or goes out of business, then the organisation will be affected. Suddenly, there could be nobody to support, upgrade, or troubleshoot the application. Such situations can be classified as IT vendor-related disasters. Suddenly a vendor's disaster now becomes the organisation's disaster, because it was dependent on their services.

How can organisations protect themselves against IT vendor-related disasters?

Organisations usually have no control over disasters relating to IT vendors, but they can minimise the effect by having more than one vendor for similar functions wherever possible. For example, organisations can buy hardware and networking equipment from different manufacturers and vendors. In the event of an IT vendor going out of business, an organisation should be in a position to speedily switch over to equivalent alternative systems from other sources. Some of the key factors to be taken into account when choosing vendors are as follows:

* Reputation of the vendor and manufacturer

* Availability of competitive products

* DR competency of the vendor

* Availability of support from third party sources.

How does one prevent IT-contractor support disasters?

Most IT contractors simply supply hardware and software, although some also provide basic support like first time installation and troubleshooting. A few of them provide detailed support and consultancy options. However, an organisation should not depend entirely on one IT contractor for all of its advice and support. It should also have qualified and knowledgeable internal members of staff to verify and understand the business pros and cons of contractors' recommendations, because a contractor may not appreciate the business implications of the recommendations. Organisations must understand that not all contractors may be qualified to give accurate business protection advice. For example, a contractor may view a hard disk crash on a critical server as a simple hard disk replacement issue, whereas it may be seen as a bankruptcy and chaos signal for the organisation if the disk wasn't being backed up regularly.

Should IT staff be outsourced?

The answer to this question is yes and no. It depends on the organisation's business management and how they view IT. Many organisations outsource their IT functions, because they view it as a burden that they can avoid, and as such, try to outsource it. Sometimes outsourcing is actually done with a herd mentality – everybody is doing it, so we should too. Other organisations view IT as a core essential function that for a variety of reasons cannot be outsourced. Either way, there are risks. For best results, IT should be a combination of internal members of staff, and some outsourced members of staff. This is because organisations can become over-zealous and decide to outsource every IT function, and this is when trouble starts. If every IT function is outsourced, there will be nobody within the organisation with the required technical expertise to verify or certify whether the outsourcing organisation is actually delivering what they have committed to. Therefore, although there are some cost advantages with outsourcing, after considering various factors a balanced approach should be taken.

Some of the pros and cons of outsourcing are as follows:

- Outsourcing decisions are usually based simply on cost factors, that is, the cheapest quote will get the order. Six months down the line, or during renewal, if another contractor quotes less that quote may get the order.

- Contractors may or may not have the expected loyalty, dedication, and commitment to a serviced organisation's business functions.

- Inadequate service level agreements (SLAs) or none at all, can cause painful legal problems when there are more important IT service issues to be worrying about.

- Outsourcing contractors usually rotate members of staff between different companies, and smooth transitions are rare. For example, there could be a disconnection between the outsourced staff that provided support between the months of January and March, versus the new outsourced staff who will provide support between April and June.

- The best members of staff at the outsourcing organisation may be placed at the premises of the best paying clients.

- Information security and confidentiality will become a serious issue, because an outsourced member of staff will have access to internal information.

- During a change-over of outsourcing contractors, the hand-over of responsibilities from one contractor to another can be a serious issue. The outgoing contractor may not carry out a proper handover to the next contractor, because the account doesn't matter to them anymore.

- Outsourced members of IT staff usually go strictly by the book or within scope of contract, and will rarely be flexible without additional costs. For example, if there is a need for them to be present in the organisation after normal working hours, or at weekends, for some urgent work, it will usually involve additional hourly costs.

- Many organisations think that by outsourcing work they are ridding themselves of the internal responsibility. However, the work must be monitored to ensure that it's progressing as expected – even though its outsourced work, it can't completely outsource the obligation to make sure everything is progressing smoothly. If all goes well with the outsourcer, there isn't much work to do. However, very often the outsourcer doesn't perform to expectations, and then there's a bigger problem to manage. Remember that contractor problems eventually become client problems.

- Other factors, such as the location of the outsourcing organisation, travel distances, holidays and internal problems all affect a client organisation.

What can be outsourced?

It depends on the nature of the organisation and the availability, or non-availability, of certain in-house skills. Other factors, such as costs, logistics and security also play an important role. Usually defence and military establishments prefer not to outsource, and expect to have qualified in-house personnel to handle everything. Some organisations may like to outsource everything as they feel they don't have, or can't afford to have expensive qualified members of IT staff on their payrolls. Frequently outsourced areas of work include the following:

- **Desktop and server hardware support:** An organisation's internal members of technical staff may not have the necessary skills to repair or replace various types of failed or new hardware. This can be outsourced and will mainly involve repairing or replacing failed hardware and setting up new hardware. Depending on the speed necessary, spares and IT staff can be external or based on-site.

- **Networking:** When organisations grow, or set up new premises, the entire place has to be wired with data and voice cables necessary for local and wide area networking. It doesn't make financial sense to have qualified in-house members of staff with those skills, and the job can easily be outsourced to reputable contractor to wire up a building.

- **Turnkey projects:** An organisation may want to establish a branch office in a different location or city. Therefore, the entire project of cabling, networking, installation of new equipment and power can be outsourced to a reputable organisation that can complete and hand over the project for a fixed fee within a fixed timeframe.

Whatever the reason for outsourcing, an organisation must consider the availability of critical support, spares and skills required for ensuring DR and BC. Clear SLAs outlining a detailed scope of work, expectations, roles and responsibilities must be enforced to cover all preventable risks.

Questions to ask vendors

When one or more vendors go out of business, an organisation must be able to locate another vendor to maintain the service to its end-users as quickly as possible. It's always better to have more than one vendor for any product or service. The following are examples of the questions to ask when selecting contractors for critical equipment or services.

- Do they have enough trained support personnel to handle technical support?

- Can every support person be contacted easily?

- Do they have adequate stock of critical spares?

- Do they have a 24x7 support option?

- Do they have a DR or BC plan, and what is it?

- Can they provide good references to verify and/or any other testimonials or certification?

Is it necessary to have contracts with vendors?

If an organisation is using external vendors to support or maintain its critical equipment and services, it's absolutely necessary to have a proper contract or SLA signed and agreed by both parties. It should be prepared in detail, and should cover the following:

- Scope of work

- Exclusions

- Roles and responsibilities

- Service hours

- Duration of contract
- Spares support
- Reports to be provided
- Payment terms
- Penalties for non-adherence.

Contracts should be prepared with the input from internal members of staff from the technical, financial and legal departments, so that all aspects are properly covered and accurately worded. If necessary, a contract must be able to withstand scrutiny by lawyers or the courts. In addition, a detailed technical SLA is also necessary to ensure proper support, and periodic audits should be conducted to ensure that the SLAs are being met.

What are the key elements of a maintenance contract or an SLA?

As already mentioned, it is necessary to have proper written agreements with vendors, service providers and consultants that are responsible for maintaining critical services for an organisation. Without a clear, signed agreement it is not possible to ensure or expect that the required assistance will be provided by external parties for essential activities in various situations.

A general purpose SLA will normally cover the points listed below. Each point needs to be elaborated in clear and definitive terms for the area of coverage. Additional items can be added depending on the organisation's specific nature of work or industry. The points are as follows:

- Name of the project or area of support

- Contract number or reference number with date
- Start date and end date for contract
- Description of the project or work expected
- Parties to the agreement, including authorised persons, departments and workplace addresses
- Detailed scope of work
- Common obligations - both parties
- Out of scope - both parties
- Assumptions, constraints, risks and limitations
- Hardware, software, spares and other requirements
- Legal aspects, jurisdiction and non-disclosure clauses
- Financials, budgets, payment terms, penalties, additional costs, extra charges, taxes and billing methods
- Standard working hours, or service windows covering number of hours per day and holidays
- Number of members of staff required on-site or on call
- Training requirements
- Out of hours work, for example, weekend work; if any.
- Help desk or support procedures, turn-around times for response, resolutions and workarounds
- Incident and problem management procedures
- Escalation procedures
- Change management procedures

- Reports and metrics (what standard reports will be exchanged)

- Project termination clauses and notice periods for closure

- Signatures of authorised representatives from both parties.

Example: An IT service *without* a maintenance contract

IT Support: 'Hello ABC Computer Organisation? We are calling from RockSolid Corp. One of our main server's power supplies has failed. Can you replace it immediately?'

ABC Organisation: 'Can you tell me the serial number of the server?'

IT Support: 'It's QW1246.'

ABC Organisation: 'Sorry, that server is out of warranty, and also not under any support maintenance agreement, so we will not be able to replace the power supply.'

Example: An IT service *with* a maintenance contract

IT Support: 'Hello ABC Computer Organisation? We are calling from RockSolid Corp. One of our main server's power supplies has failed. Can you replace it immediately?'

ABC Organisation: 'Can you tell me the serial number of the

---

server?'

IT Support: 'It's QW1246.'

ABC Organisation: 'Thank you for the details. That server is under our maintenance contract. We will replace the power supply within the next four hours.'

CHAPTER 9: IT PROJECT FAILURES

'Mr Corleone is a man who insists on hearing all bad news immediately.'

The Godfather

What is an IT project?

An organisation may require a myriad of IT equipment, such as computers, telecom devices, data and voice lines, security devices, firewalls and software. Proper selection, installation, configuration, and maintenance of IT environments are of crucial importance, and the implementation, configuration and handover of the equipment can be considered as an IT project. For example, installing a new LAN with the necessary servers, e-mail, internet, desktops and preloaded software for a new office can be classified as an IT project. Many factors must be considered during an IT implementation. Some of the most common and important factors to be considered in an IT project are as follows:

- Proper selection of the right equipment

- Design and capacity planning

- Cost factors and budgets (one-off and ongoing)

- Inter-dependencies

- Software licensing issues

- Ongoing support, maintenance and staffing issues

- Training and support requirements
- External factors
- Contractor contracts
- Miscellaneous issues

Many organisations outsource their internal IT work, and may also serve as service providers to external clients. As pre-mentioned, organisations are heavily dependent on external service providers to implement, maintain and support their IT infrastructure. They may also outsource entire IT projects to external service providers and consultants.

IT projects can fail in a number of ways, and such failures can have a severe impact on an organisation as outlined below.

Costs: Improperly designed or poorly-chosen equipment can result in a lot of wasted costs.

Reputation losses: Failure to implement an IT project that meets a customer's requirements can cause reputation losses for the service provider, as well as losses for the client. For example, poor project deliveries to customers can affect an organisation's reputation, causing loss of new or existing customers.

Legal issues: Customers may also sue service providers if they make a mistake with critical projects. For example, external customers may sue software development companies for delaying or messing up the implementation of a critical software project.

These are all disasters from a business perspective.

Why do IT projects fail?

As with any project, there are a number of risks associated with an IT project, and they are more likely to affect an organisation than non-IT project. This is because they are more and more dependent on IT for all their data, communications and connectivity. Furthermore, organisations have to constantly upgrade and implement newer and newer technologies to remain competitive, and the implementation of such technologies will normally involve constantly creating and managing new IT projects. However, there are many reasons why such projects fail.

- **Poor capacity planning:** Certain multi-user data entry software may not be able to handle heavy data entry loads. Or a new network connection between offices may not be able to handle the level of data traffic between the sites.

- **Bad technical designs:** It is possible for an entire IT project to have a bad technical design. For example, service providers or IT departments may select incorrect or unsuitable IT equipment, due to budget constraints, insufficient knowledge, sales gimmicks and attractive marketing brochures. The entire design may be technically flawed, or may not be the right solution for the need. In such cases, the technical implementation may be successful, but later, it may not meet business requirements.

- **Political reasons:** To some degree, no organisation is free from internal politics. In addition, there are more culture clashes as workforces become more and more culturally diverse. A project initiated by an organisation's head of office located in one country may cause job losses to members of staff situated in another. Such projects risk failure, or delay, caused by staff of service providers who may be negatively affected.

- **Budgets and timelines:** Projects can also fail to meet an organisation's business expectations due to inadequate budgets or unrealistic timelines.

- **Poor management:** According to various workplace surveys and studies, poor management is accountable for a large percentage of project failures. This can include poor knowledge, inadequate experience, or lack of professionalism - all of which can lead to various kinds of workplace and team disorders. Poor management can cause projects to fail by causing resignations of key talented members of staff, unachievable deadlines, or over-commitments. Believe it or not, many members of staff prefer not to report potential problems to senior management, either because they don't want to appear to have failed, or because of bad experiences in the past. Many managers don't like to hear bad or expensive news, and very often a 'shoot the messenger' attitude is displayed instead of appreciating the gesture. Therefore, members of staff may avoid or delay telling their managers bad news, which may result in catastrophes later.

- **Business decisions:** In many medium to high profile projects, the objectives, scope, budgets, timelines and people are usually decided at very senior levels of management. Such projects are then pushed downwards through the organisation with a tremendous amount of pressure. Senior management may refuse to accept or listen to any real-world issues, or specific problems that might affect the project. Messengers of bad news may be pushed out of the projects, leading to a fear psychosis, covering up of bad news and cost escalations. Often bad news that is identified at the lower levels gets sugar-coated and presented as a non-issue, or even good news to senior management. Soon reality kicks in, and it will be too late to prevent the impending project failures.

- **Organisational inadequacies:** Not all organisations are capable of flawless project execution within agreed costs and timeframes, and it doesn't matter about the size of the organisation. Sometimes a larger organisation may not be able to fulfil the needs of a small organisation, because of the inherent way in which the larger one functions. Long timeframes, elaborate processes and lavish overheads may cause lots of grief to a small organisation. Conversely, a smaller organisation may not have the resources and bandwidth to handle IT projects for a large conglomerate.

- **External factors:** Projects can also fail due to external factors beyond the control of the organisation, for example, political disturbances, contractor issues or regulatory issues.

How can organisations avoid IT project failures?

In spite of significant progress with project management methodologies, best practices and the availability of new technologies, the success rates of medium to large scale IT projects are still poor. Many projects do not meet the original cost and other benefits assumed or predicted at the beginning. The rest are either cancelled completely, delayed beyond acceptable limits, over-budget, or go completely haywire and don't even meet the organisation's minimum business or functional requirements.

IT projects are always technology related, and can be simple or extremely complex. The quirk of IT projects is that if the projects are managed by pure technical experts they could turn out to be a great technical success, but may not meet business expectations. On the other hand, if a pure business manager runs the project it can lead to a technical failure caused by lack of expertise. It's often difficult to achieve a balance between the two, and this is where the role of a Chief Technology Officer (CTO) or a Chief Information Officer (CIO) is most important, because this role must interface between the business and technical experts for IT projects.

Some of the ways to avoid IT project disasters are as follows:

- **Understanding customer requirements:** The heart of any IT project lies in clearly understanding and documenting the customer's requirements. The requirements must be agreed in writing and clearly signed-off. Customers may not be very clear on their requirements, and may give vague or superficial requirements, and then expect something more dramatic after implementation. The trick is to get the correct requirements from the customer before the project is started. New requirements during the course of a project must also be captured and properly processed.

- **Setting achievable commitments:** In the face of competition many organisations over commit on their product or services. Such commitments will normally not be achievable due to real-world constraints. An organisation must only commit to what is really achievable under any given circumstances. Its reputation increases if they under promise and over deliver, rather than over promise and under deliver.

- **Accurate budgets:** Though it may be impossible to get approvals for a generous budget, it's absolutely necessary to have all IT related costs, such as hardware, software, telecom, installation, cables, support, upgrades, licences and other essential costs clear, with a reasonable contingency budget for each. In addition, other costs, such as taxes, transport, travel, insurance, people and fees must also be adequately covered to arrive at an overall budget. Every single cost and effort should be accurately documented, and a budget presented and approved. Provision must also be made for escalations in a contingency budget should the original requirements suddenly change for any reason.

- **Set clear project deliverables:** An IT project manager must have a clear and detailed picture of what is being achieved or delivered to a customer, or the project sponsor. Commitments must be very clear and fully understood by both parties. Large projects have a particular tendency to change track, so it's always better to involve the customer at regular intervals to ensure that the project is on track to achieving its objectives.

- **Establish an SLA:** Critical projects are often started without establishing proper documentation, which may lead to all kinds of misunderstandings and confusions later. SLAs don't prevent project failures, but they do minimise the impact of a failure due to expectations mismatch, cost factors and post implementation hassles. It's always recommended to establish a clear SLA between the customer and the service provider to ensure that every aspect of the project is covered in writing. SLAs must be prepared by involving the following departments from both sides to avoid complications and misunderstandings later:

  - Technical departments for understanding and defining the IT deliverables. Finance departments for defining the financial implications. Legal departments for understanding and minimising legal complications, should there be a legal battle later. Others - if required.

- **Killing projects on time:** Many projects run into problems for various reasons. Killing a bad project may actually save time, cost and reputation. However, it isn't an easy job to kill a project, and the members of staff working on the actual project may not be able to take such decisions. Such decisions can often only be taken by senior levels of management and to convince them to do so can be problematic. There could also be various official and political compulsions that prevent bad projects from being killed. However, it may be in the best interests of an organisation to recognise and kill bad projects on time before they cause further damage.

- **Learning from past mistakes:** Experienced project managers know that there are many things that can go wrong in spite of detailed planning. Some problems can be anticipated, but many can't. It's important to learn from mistakes and problems faced in the past. Project managers should cultivate the habit of learning from others' mistakes in order to avoid making the same mistakes themselves. For example, many organisations may routinely over commit on various aspects, and end up with problems later. IT project failures can be devastating to an organisation. Abnormal delays, virus filled software, missing features and expectation mismatches can mean the end of a project, the organisation's reputation, or even financial ruin.

- **Resource back-ups:** Projects can fail due to resignations, accidents and health issues of its key members of staff, thus adversely affecting the project. A project manager must ensure that all risks related to key people; including the project manager, are adequately covered by a suitable back-up plan. Resignation of a key member of staff is hard to prevent, but good knowledge management and role sharing would reduce the impact on the project.

- **Training:** Lack of appropriate training for members of a project team can also be a big issue. Appropriate training and qualifications, for example PRINCE2®, would also help ensure the project runs according to plan.

CHAPTER 10: INFORMATION SECURITY

'When humans are too happy, even the gods are jealous.'

Anonymous

What is information security?

An organisation may rely on several types of data for its day-to-day business functions and to compete in the market. Some of this data can be highly confidential and must not be viewed, or altered, by unauthorised persons. If such information is somehow compromised then an organisation can get into serious trouble. For example, the salary details of its members of staff shouldn't be made viewable to the public, or its payment or e-commerce website might be breached and defaced by hackers, causing damage to its reputation. It's necessary to have a protective envelope around the various kinds of data that an organisation uses. This is called information security. It prevents compromises to the integrity, confidentiality or availability of its information, and an organisation should classify all of its data appropriately, ensuring proper safeguards for each. Examples of classifying an organisation's data include the following:

- **Confidential:** Only the member of staff and certain other staff members, such as HR and finance, should know a staff member's salary - it should not be visible to others.

- **Secure or restricted:** Only authorised members of staff should handle passwords of mission critical systems, production servers, etc.

- **Internal or private:** General organisation policies can be made visible to all members of staff via its intranet.

- **Important:** A software development team can classify its software code as important, and can restrict its access to certain team members only.

- **General or public:** Certain information, such as fire safety, health tips and first aid can be classified as general and displayed for everyone to view.

What are the various ways in which information security can be compromised?

As pre-mentioned, disasters can happen to an organisation if its information security is compromised in any one of a number of the following different ways:

- Internet connections can be hacked into by unauthorised persons, if there is no proper firewall, or intrusion detection system

- . A firewall will prevent an internal IP network being visible to the outside world. An intrusion detection system will spot suspicious activities happening on the network, for example, it can detect if some rogue software program is initiating a 'denial of service' attack on a website.

- A laptop containing confidential and sensitive information could be stolen.

- Confidential documents may be scanned or photocopied by unauthorised members of staff.
- Unauthorised persons could intercept e-mail.
- Unauthorised persons may get access to data centres.
- Removable storage devices containing confidential data can fall into the wrong hands.
- External consultants and contractors working within an organisation may view or access confidential data they aren't supposed to see.
- Carelessness and human error in allowing unauthorized persons to obtain passwords.
- Critical passwords getting lost, stolen or changed by unauthorised personnel.
- A website can be hacked into and altered, or sensitive information stolen. For example, if products are sold via the Internet, the website could be hacked into and customer information, such as credit card numbers and e-mail IDs collected.
- Former members of staff may destroy important data before they leave, or pass on sensitive information to outsiders.

What safeguards are available to protect information?

There are different types of safeguard depending on the nature of an organisation. Some of the common precautions that can be taken are as follows:

- House all confidential data in a secure file server with access only by the authorised department's personnel.

Keep the administrative password in a secure safe, and all usage should be logged in a register.

- Prevent the printing, photocopying or e-mailing of certain types of documents. For example, it's possible to convert many types of document into an Adobe PDF file and have printing disabled to make it read-only.

- Ensure that all hard copies of confidential documents are shredded after use, so that they don't fall into the hands of unauthorised persons.

- Ensure that no important data is stored on laptops or removable storage devices that can easily get misplaced or stolen.

- Implement electronic systems to log and monitor activities on all computers, or restrict access to certain users.

- Monitor the internet access of every member of staff and ensure there is no access to chat sites or other non-business sites.

- If possible, prevent internet and external e-mail access to certain highly sensitive job profiles in order to prevent details, for example, those of a customer's credit card, falling into the wrong hands.

- Prevent users from bringing smartphones, digital cameras and other communication gadgets into the organisation.

- Information security is a very wide topic and encompasses several areas. It is recommended that this should be the responsibility of a separate department in within an organisation.

CHAPTER 11: CYBER SECURITY ISSUES

'It's only when they go wrong, that machines remind you how powerful they are.'

Clive James

What is Cyber Security?

Cyber security is information security principles applied to an organisation's computers and networks. It contains technologies and processes designed to protect computers, networks and data from unauthorised access, vulnerabilities and attacks routed via the Internet by cyber criminals.

Who is a Cyber Criminal?

A cyber criminal is someone who commits crimes using computers, internet and software. These criminals attack computers, individuals or organisations to perform malicious activities, such as spreading viruses, data theft, identity theft, fraud or to steal sensitive data. Cyber criminals have come a long way from being mischievous individuals to government sponsored organisations who use it for espionage or electronic terrorism on other countries. Cyber crime is now a billion dollar industry and cyber criminals come in various forms like expert programmers, IT specialists, hackers, organised mafia, government agencies, etc. Today most organisations are networked internally and externally. As a result of this cyber criminals can wreak havoc on an organisation if they get unauthorised access into the systems. Some of the ways in which an organisation can be crippled are listed as follows.

- Plain mischief like deleting files or causing computer to crash

- Theft of sensitive data useful for competitors or for blackmail

- Disabling or crippling a network, for example of an electrical grid or a military organisation.

- Espionage activities by competitors or even from rogue countries.

What is hacking?

Hacking is gaining unauthorised access to a computer, its files and programs, and the people who do this are called hackers. Hacking may happen simply for fun, or for commercial gain. For example, a competitor may hack into an organisation's network and gain access to critical or sensitive information. Sometimes hackers may destroy or copy important data, or do something worse. For example, to rob a bank in the past would either have been done so physically, creating risk, or by an excellent forger. Today it isn't even necessary to visit a bank to rob it, and it can easily be done without raising any alarms for weeks. So how is it easy for criminals to rob a bank? The simple answer is the Internet. Many aspects of people's lives, such as banking, purchases and communications depend on the Internet and worldwide connectivity. While the Internet offers several conveniences, it can also ruin lives in an instant through identity theft, online scams and other threats. A thief that knows a lot about modern technology can simply sit in comfort and leisurely hack into a bank's computer system using software to steal money or create havoc by changing numbers on bank accounts. While this may be an example of plain theft or mischief, the Internet can also be used to facilitate much bigger crimes. Worldwide, many organisations get hacked into, and many don't even realise it has happened, because they won't have the required expertise to detect it. Sometimes the hacking can be harmless, but it can also be deadly and even ruin an organisation. For example, the hacking of the Sony Play Station network in 2011 caused a great amount of damage and annoyance to millions of users. The breach also led to the theft of the data of more than 70 million users, and it took Sony several days to restore and fix the system. Sony is not alone. Every time someone makes an online purchase, visits a website or carries out an online banking transaction they are exposing themselves to risk.

How do hackers operate?

Some of the common ways computers can be broken into or disabled by hackers are as follows:

Password theft: A password is simply a string of keyboard characters, which a person must remember and type into a computer terminal when required. There are several methods for cracking a password. Specialised password cracking software packages are available that can crack a password using dictionary attacks, brute force attacks and hybrid attacks.

Trojan horses: A Trojan horse is malicious software surreptitiously delivered inside a computer. Trojan horses can be programs that destroy hard drives, corrupt files, record keystrokes, monitor network traffic, track web usage, allow remote control, transmit data files to others, launch attacks against other targets, and more. All a Trojan horse attack needs to be successful is a single user to execute the program. Once that is accomplished, the malicious software is automatically launched, often without any symptoms of unwanted activity. A Trojan horse could be delivered via e-mail as an attachment, or it could be presented on a website as a download. Protection lies in malicious code detection tools, modern anti-virus protection, other forms of malware scanners and user education.

Denial of service: Sometimes a hacker uses a network of computers to sabotage a specific website or server. The idea is to make all the computers contact a specific server or website repeatedly. The sudden increase in traffic can cause the site to become very slow, or simply collapse. Sometimes the traffic is enough to shut it down completely. This is called a Denial of Service (DoS) attack.

Exploiting settings: Attacking a target network or computer is easier when that target is using the defaults set by the manufacturer. Many attack tools and scripts assume that the target is configured using the default settings. One of the effective security precautions is simply to change the defaults. It's the user's responsibility to know about the defaults of the hardware and software products used, and change those defaults to custom settings. The more customised the configurations and settings, the more the system will be incompatible with attack tools and exploitation scripts.

Defacing websites: A fairly common form of external attack is website defacing. An organisation's website can be defaced and nonsense information displayed. This attack uses password cracking to penetrate websites that the attacker wants to deface. A common way to get into a website is by a dictionary attack. A dictionary file (a text file full of dictionary words) is loaded into a cracking application, which is run against common user accounts used by the application or website login. Because the majority of passwords are often simplistic, running a dictionary attack is often sufficient to do the job.

Packet sniffing: Packet sniffer is an application that captures data packets, and can be used to capture passwords and other data in transit over the network.

Key loggers: These are programs that record keystrokes made by a user, allowing hackers to discover passwords and login codes.

Rootkits and Backdoors: Rootkits are a collection of programs that permit administrator-level control of a computer. Hackers use rootkits to control computers and evade detection. Backdoors are methods of circumventing the normal operating system procedures, allowing a hacker to access information on another computer.

Spoofing attack (Phishing): A spoofing attack usually involves a program, system or website masquerading as another, thereby being treated as a trusted system by a user or another program. The purpose of this is usually to fool programs, systems or users into revealing confidential information to the attacker, for example, user names and passwords.

Vulnerability scanner: A vulnerability scanner is a tool used to check computers and networks for known weaknesses. Hackers also commonly use port scanners. These check to identify which ports on a specified computer are 'open' or available to access the computer. In the event that 'open' ports are discovered, smart programmers can access the computer or network and cause havoc.

How can an organisation prevent hacking?

Some of the ways that an organisation can prevent hacking include:

- Have internal and external systems periodically audited for risks and technical loopholes by reputable cyber security experts. Implement all suggestions to close the technical loopholes. For example, implement best practices for secure configurations of computers, servers, network equipment and mobile devices

- Install a state of the art firewall (hardware or software or both) between the organisation's network and the Internet. Firewalls prevent a hacker sitting on the Internet from snooping into an organisation's network.

- Install all of the manufacturer's recommended patches, hot fixes and service packs on computers. These fix various vulnerabilities that can be exploited to hack into a machine.

- Log all accesses into and out of a network using special tools that can detect which computer accessed a system. For example, with the latest logging tools available it's possible to identify the exact IP address and other details of the computer that accessed a credit card system. It's even possible to pinpoint it if it's located in another country.

- Change critical passwords often and ensure that they aren't easy to guess. For example, don't name the passwords 'blank', 'password', 'secret', or names that are easy to guess. Use a combination of alpha-numeric, symbols and uppercase/lowercase characters.

- Always have the latest anti-virus software installed on all critical systems.

- Install spyware and adware removers. Spyware and adware are tiny programs that install themselves without permission of the user while browsing the Web. Anti-virus programs usually can't detect such programs. Depending on how it's written, adware and spyware can send out sensitive information without the user's knowledge.

- Don't open suspicious e-mail attachments, because they may contain a Trojan virus or a program designed to wreak havoc on a computer. Websites designed by troublemakers provide software which is intentionally designed to hack into and damage a computer.

- Have a detailed cyber security audit conducted periodically through reputed cyber security companies. They will have the necessary tools and knowledge to pinpoint all the loopholes, open ports, etc., of various IT equipment and software used in an organisation. Once done implement all their recommendations.

Exploring Cloud services

With the advent of new technologies it's no longer necessary for an organisation to own all the hardware and software necessary for their business. Today there are qualified service providers that will help outsource most of its technical needs. For example, it's no longer necessary for it to install and maintain an e-mail server or many other types of servers in-house. An external contractor will be able to provide an e-mail service by hosting a mail service on the Internet, customised to the organisation's needs. Similarly, there are service providers who will provide many applications, such as finance applications, databases and storage drives. Such services are called cloud services and an investment in hardware within an organisation would be minimal, that is, all data and applications will be on in the Cloud. While this may sound very convenient for a business manager who may want to avoid the trouble of having equipment and employing service personnel in-house, such cloud services may bring new problems. For example, if there is an outsourced mail service, then an organisation will no longer have full control over it, and if the service provider goes bankrupt, or gets hacked into, then dozens of companies who depend on their services may lose contact with their customers. Therefore, an organisation should choose cloud services carefully and have extensive discussions with the service providers to ensure its information isn't hacked or compromised. It shouldn't opt in simply because it's the latest trend, because reversing decisions can often be costly and troublesome if things don't work as expected. But, according to industry experts, cloud services are the way of the future once the right security practices are implemented.

CHAPTER 12: INTRODUCTION TO NON-IT DISASTERS

'There are two big forces at work, external and internal. We have very little control over external forces such as tornadoes, earthquakes, floods, disasters, illness and pain. What really matters is the internal force. How do I respond to those disasters? Over that I have complete control.'

Leo Buscaglia

What are some of the non-IT disasters that could affect an organisation?

The aim of this chapter is not to cover every conceivable disaster comprehensively. Rather, it's to raise awareness about the type of disaster that could befall an organisation, prompt it to analyse the specific risks faced, and to encourage it to include the most relevant scenarios in its DRP and BCP.

Every department within an organisation will have its own importance and dependency on others, and each must function collaboratively to ensure continued revenues and future business. Major equipment failures aren't the only disasters that can happen – they can happen in many other areas as well. Risks and potential disasters lurk everywhere. Some of the non-IT disasters that can strike an organisation are as follows:

- Human errors
- Project failures

- Marketing and sales blunders

- Numerous other disasters.

What is a human error?

Human errors happen when people do something they are not supposed to do, either deliberately, or by mistake. Myriads of human errors are possible, from both management and members of staff, and account for thousands of small to gigantic disasters. A technician may simply use a wrong computer command and wipe out years of data in seconds, or an electrician may accidentally cross some wires and blow up the entire electrical system. Human errors and their impact can be minimised as follows:

- Keep things simple and have clear labels on mission critical equipment.

- Have only authorised and trained members of staff to handle sensitive functions.

- Provide adequate training for all members of staff.

- Provide user education - 'dos and don'ts'.

- Follow professional management practices. For example, a bold decision by the management to hastily dismiss a popular member of staff may result in abrupt union problems and the factory being set on fire. There was a particular case in India where a brash factory owner slapped a popular, knowledgeable member of staff over a disagreement regarding increasing production. As the news spread the local and external labour unions got involved and shut the factory. During a skirmish, miscreants damaged some expensive equipment and set fire to the stores resulting in millions of lost rupees, and factory downtime for a couple of months.

Every human error is a learning opportunity: make the most of it. Analyse it and take all necessary steps to prevent a recurrence, not just of that particular error, but of ones like it. Then be grateful that as a result of that particular member of staff's blunder, the organisation is more robust. Therefore, no action should be taken against them unless their action was malicious.

What are marketing and sales errors?

To tackle today's business world of high competition, many organisations resort to every trick in the book to lure customers to their services and products. Ever-increasing business pressures lead to members of marketing and sales staff promising the moon to every potential customer they meet, which can later result in serious business issues.

What are financial disasters?

A financial disaster is anything that seriously and negatively affects an organisation's revenues. Any of the other disasters discussed in this book can have a negative financial impact, but something that worries a Chief Financial Officer (CFO) most is exposure to fraud. In some large scale financial scandals the CFO, Chief Executive Officer (CEO) and other senior managers may be directly and knowingly involved. Fraud comes in many different guises:

- Members of staff cheating the organisation, perhaps through an invoicing scam using a partner outside the organisation to help them.

- Suppliers cheating the organisation, perhaps through over-billing or supplying sub-specification materials.

- Customers cheating the organisation, such as simply not paying.

- Senior management cheating the organisation – and everybody else. The Enron scandal in the US led to the downfall of not only the organisation (with members of staff losing pensions as well as jobs), but also of their accountants. This in turn led to the Sarbanes-Oxley Act, more regulation for American companies and de-listings from the New York Stock Exchange.

Every organisation must ensure that its financial systems, processes and policies are in proper order and within legal limits and government regulations.[1]

What are some of the common recruitment risks?

This is not a new type of disaster. There was a time when an organisation would only hire highly trained and educated people who knew their stuff, or would hire trainees and train them to the fullest possible extent. For example, it used to be unusual for anyone to be promoted to the position of a manager until they had worked for some years and understood the trade properly. Nowadays, it isn't always necessary to have any real experience to become a senior manager in charge of a complex project. Hiring the wrong people can cause various types of disaster. A bad

---

[1] This, of course, is known as 'corporate governance'. For more information on this subject, as well as a range of interesting books, *see* www.itgovernance.co.uk/corporate_governance.aspx.

mannered or unprofessional manager or supervisor can affect staff member's morale and customer satisfaction.

Improper people management could lead to the following issues:

- Good and experienced members of staff may resign due to poor supervisors.

- Members of staff who don't put customer care first may cause business losses or even lawsuits.

- Staff harassment and workplace bullying can lead to reputation losses or hefty lawsuits.

All of these can be described as recruitment disasters that eventually affect the organisation.

How do you handle fire related disasters?

A fire can wipe out years of work within minutes and hours. Hence, organisations must ensure they have the maximum fire prevention methods. Some of the ways to prevent fire related disasters are as follows.

- Have plenty of fire extinguishers around and frequently test that they're working.

- Train as many members of staff as possible to operate a fire extinguisher.

- For areas where it's possible, have automatic or manual water sprinklers installed.

- Always keep overhead tanks and fire hydrants in working condition.

- Ensure that nobody parks vehicles, or loads material near fire extinguishers, fire hydrants, water supply, etc.

- Have the building and offices inspected by the fire service and other qualified consultants regularly and implement their recommendations.

- Have enough fire exits all around and keep their pathways free.

- Ban smoking on the premises. Don't allow fireworks during celebrations.

- Have electrical equipment tested and certified frequently.

- Inspect and remove all inflammable material throughout the organisation.

- Install fire alarms and keep them in working condition.

- Practice fire drill and evacuation procedures regularly.

What about health and biological threats to an organisation's members of staff?

This is a serious concern among some organisations and must be handled carefully, especially in companies that deal with chemicals. We are not referring to a terrorist or biological weapons attack on an organisation here, but biological attacks that happen due to unhygienic conditions or improper care. An organisation must ensure that its water supply, air-conditioners, etc. are subject to periodic checks to ensure that there are no health related risks. If the drinking water supply tank gets polluted or infected with a bacteria or virus, the entire staff force can quickly become seriously sick. If the cooling towers or evaporative condensers are harbouring bacteria then people can catch the fatal Legionnaire's disease. For an extreme example, in the 1980s a deadly gas leak in the Union Carbide factory in

India killed and injured thousands of people in the factory and its surroundings.

Some of the common methods to keep the organisation safe from such threats are listed below:

- Check the water supply periodically to ensure clean filtered water is supplied everywhere.

- Keep all hazardous materials and chemicals in recommended containers.

- Ensure that the building's members of security staff are trained in all emergency first aid procedures.

- Have telephone numbers of doctors and hospitals easily accessible and updated.

- An organisation that manufactures chemicals, explosives and medicines must have very, very strict safety guidelines to ensure their own members of staff, as well as the entire surroundings, are protected from harmful effects.

- Ensure compliance with all health and safety regulations and legislation. If in doubt about what regulations apply to an organisation – find out. (In the UK the best starting point is the Health and Safety Executive: *www.hse.gov.uk*).

What about electrical failures and blackouts?

All organisations need electricity to function. Electricity is the lifeblood of many organisations, and electrical faults and blackouts account for a large percentage of disasters worldwide. A simple short circuit in a factory can set the whole factory ablaze. Lengthy power failures or blackouts also affect an organisation's business. Electricity can kill and injure people if not handled with care, so organisations must ensure that their electrical systems are always in perfect working condition. Some of the common methods to prevent electrical disasters are listed below:

- Have the building wired by professional electricians.

- Ensure that all electrical equipment has the necessary fuses, overload trippers, safety handles and insulations.

- Don't have loose wires hanging around.

- Ensure that electrical points and wiring blocks are safely shielded from unauthorised personnel.

- Ensure there's no water seepage near electrical items.

- Ensure the cables and connectors used are of high quality, even though they may be expensive. Loose connections and faulty connectors are the number one cause of electrical failures.

- Have qualified electricians inspect and certify the building wiring systems.

- When equipment is not in use don't leave it powered on. Switch off all unnecessary electrical gadgets when leaving the premises.

- Have proper UPS and generators for critical equipment.

- Always draw the recommended amount of power. Never short-circuit fuses just to draw more power.

- Have torches, batteries and emergency lights at all required places.

- Use a certified electrical consultant for best results.

What precautions can an organisation take to handle civil disturbances?

Civil disturbances are quite common in many countries. Unemployment, religious attacks, over-population, terrorism, religious processions and political causes can all lead to civil disturbances. Agitated crowds can easily set fire to a building or vehicles or attack innocent people. The frenzy of an agitated crowd cannot be controlled easily.

An organisation can ensure some degree of control over, and protection from, civil disturbances by following these measures:

- At the first sign of a civil disturbance, ensure the police and fire service are called to protect the building, members of staff and other property.

- If possible, send all members of staff home, or to safe locations using all available means of transport to prevent injuries to them if a riot starts suddenly.

- Tell members of staff not to try any heroics or unnecessary engagement with the rioters.

- Follow all recommendations offered by the police and fire service.

- If a riot happens, if possible, ensure that no member of staff is harmed. If they are, ensure they receive urgent medical treatment.

How can an organisation take precaution against terrorism?

Terrorism is spreading worldwide at an alarming rate A few, unguaranteed, methods of avoiding terrorism are as follows:

- If possible, ensure that the organisation does not have main branches or large offices in states and countries prone to terrorism.

- Assess countries and geographical locations by order of safety in terms of crime, terrorism, political turmoil, and religious preferences, and ensure only the minimum amount of members of staff and property are exposed to such risks.

- Constantly assess risks and political scenarios to evacuate members of staff if necessary. There are reputable consultancies that specialise in this sort of analysis.

- If possible, ensure that members of staff don't take their families to political and other religious hotspots.

- Hire and train people from the local community as members of staff.

- If possible, keep good relations with local politicians. This is really helpful in many third world countries where political parties wield enormous power over the business community.

- In areas where terrorism and crime are rampant, try to indulge in charitable works and offer more employment for local people. Organisations must develop a social and community approach to generating more jobs. More and more employment means less and less crime, trouble and other disturbances on the streets.

- Have highly trained security guards and protection forces wherever possible and where necessary.

What is a travel-related risk?

In the past business travel was considered a luxury. It still retains some of its past glory, but travel nowadays is considered a risk. The increase in terrorist threats, civil disturbances, airport security, global unrest and political instability contributes to travel related risk. It's difficult to travel peacefully on any business trip without considering the numerous risks associated with it. Terrorists have attacked planes, airports and train stations, killing and injuring hundreds of passengers. Today, business people prefer to avoid travel unless it's absolutely essential. International travellers face a variety of threats that can disrupt a business trip, along with personal risk. Getting stranded in an alien country with little knowledge of local issues or escape routes can be devastating to anyone on a business trip. In view of the risks, organisations and governments are classifying countries and states into various categories that will be helpful in deciding whether to go on a business trip or not. Some of the common classifications are listed in *Table 5*.

Table 5: Travel-related risks

Country	Low risk	Medium risk	High risk
A	–	Crime, violence and theft	–
B	–	–	Terrorism, bombs, continuous conflict, war
C	Avoid crowded places; poor medical treatment	–	–

Many insurance organisations offer insurance and evacuation services for certain sensitive countries. In the event of an emergency, the insurance holder can dial a free-phone number and receive immediate assistance in the foreign country. Risk assessment teams are being formed in various organisations whose main business is to constantly assess various types of travel and other risks to the organisation.

Some of the common methods to minimise travel-related risks are as follows:

- Avoid business travel in groups. Split the group and take different routes or flights.

- Use video-conferencing wherever possible, particularly to avoid short trips.

- Use a reputable travel agent and get the complete itinerary down to the smallest detail.

- Study the political conditions of the destination countries before travelling.

- Follow all rules and regulations of the host country.

- Keep all medicines and emergency numbers to hand. Always carry a reputable mobile phone with international roaming facility enabled. Remember to carry its charger and a multi-socket connector for different countries.

- If possible, memorise telephone numbers, addresses, and e-mail IDs.

- Don't travel without identification papers and local contact telephone numbers.

- Always arrange for some reliable local help through the travel agent.

- Avoid travelling independently in foreign countries. Always take some trustworthy local help if possible.

For further information on business travel hazards consult the country's embassy in the destination country.

What are the usual trade or labour union problems?

Many organisations and factories worldwide have strong trade or labour unions. These are necessary in many types of organisations to keep a check on unfair labour practices or exploitation of workers by management. On the other hand, they can also paralyse an organisation's business 'at the drop of a hat'- sometimes for trivial reasons. In some parts of the world disputes get out of hand and the union members resort to violence and damage to equipment. An organisation can go bankrupt if the labour unions don't listen to reason, but equally the management shouldn't simply ride roughshod over their workers. In many countries there are strict laws governing on what trade unions and employers can and can't do. However, despite such laws, strikes are still surprisingly common. According to the latest government figures in the UK, 50 days are lost each year per 1,000 members of staff, and even more so elsewhere. Strikes are simply the most extreme symptom of industrial relation problems. The following lists precautions that an organisation can take to minimise exposure to such problems. It's not exhaustive, but depending on the issues and practices in the part of the world where the organisation is located, it will give an idea of the precautions it may consider taking:

- Have proper and transparent HR polices for all members of staff.

- Provide proper and reasonable benefits for members of staff, such as medical facilities, transport, etc.

- Have a proper profit-sharing scheme for members of staff.

- Treat all members of staff with respect & dignity.

- Follow all established legal procedures while hiring and firing members of staff.

- Provide members of staff with adequate financial support during critical illness.

- Have proper background checks to ensure that managers and supervisors treat members of staff and workers with respect.

- Implement all guidelines and safeguards pertaining to the specific industry.

What about the psychological effects of a disaster on members of staff?

Depending on its nature, a disaster can have a severe psychological impact on an organisation's members of staff. During a crisis situation, personnel and family matters take priority over resuming business as usual. For example, if there is a fire and many staff are hurt or badly burnt, it will not be possible for them to ignore their personal suffering and start concentrating on DR or BC. An organisation must be prepared to handle the psychological factors associated with a disaster. They should first ensure that the welfare and safety of its staff takes priority over instant DR and worrying about losses in productivity. DR and BC must be as humane as possible. Every effort must also be made to ensure that members of staff continue to receive their wages or acceptable salaries in the event of a major disaster.

What is a reputational risk?

In today's highly competitive business environment, an organisation's reputation in the eyes of a customer or stakeholder is extremely important. Reputation sells an organisation's products and services, and its loss can harm it in very severe ways. For example, famous and powerful organisations, such as Arthur Andersen and Enron, collapsed because of reputational issues. Often, it's not necessary for an organisation to commit a serious crime for its reputation to take a plunge. A single case of harassment of a member of staff by one of its managers can cause irreparable damage to an organisation if leaked to the media. A false and unproven allegation in the newspapers by a reporter can also cause severe damage. For example, if a car owner lodges a legal case against a car manufacturer alleging that the brakes are faulty, and this attracts publicity, then the organisation's business can drop drastically - even though it could be a one-off case of a brake failure in a single car. An organisation must guard its reputation very, very carefully in order to remain in business. Even the best public relations (PR) managers can't rectify a ruined reputation. Here are suggested ways to safeguard an organisation's reputation:

- Members of staff must be trained and informed not to divulge anything about the organisation to outsiders. For example, only the authorised press representative or the crisis management team must be allowed to speak to the media regarding any organisation issues.

- Ensure that its commitments to customers are met in accordance with their promises.

- Study customer complaints and handle them appropriately and in a timely manner.

- Ensure that unauthorised persons or other organisations don't use their names, trademarks, logos, etc., directly or indirectly, without permission.

- Ensure that it follows professional, legal and other formalities. For example, adequate safeguards must be in place to ensure that there's no harassment of any sorts to any of its department's members of staff.

- Incidents that have the potential to blow out of proportion must be handled speedily and effectively. For example, if there is an unacceptable rumour floating around about its products or services, then it should immediately contact the media explaining the organisation's position.

- Have proper non-disclosure agreements with contractors, suppliers and consultants with strict penalties to prevent leaks of inside information. If an organisation is too small to have a PR department, or if its existing members of PR staff or consultants don't have experience of crisis management, then it should identify a PR consultant who specialises in this field. Have them prepare a crisis management communication plan, and agree with them under what circumstances and at what cost they would be able to act. If senior management are worried that the organisation is in danger of an imminent collapse unless something can be done about the media reports, it is not the time to start thinking about finding a PR consultant and negotiating a fee with them – they're wanted in the office within the hour, helping sort out the crisis.

What about industrial espionage?

Industrial espionage is the theft, spying on, or sabotage of an organisation's confidential information by competitors, other countries, or spies. Industrial espionage isn't restricted to James Bond movies, but is all around. An example of industrial espionage could be a car manufacturer that's secretly stealing designs of new car models from another manufacturer. Industrial espionage is very difficult to control with the easy availability of e-mail, tiny storage devices, etc. A member of staff could easily steal many confidential documents, expensive designs, etc.

from an organisation and sell it to a competitor. Mobile phones and easy internet access provide opportunities, or somebody could steal a laptop containing sensitive information and within seconds, leak the organisation's secrets. Members of staff who may be secretly working for personal gain or competitors may also commit espionage activities.

A reputable organisation can easily become bankrupt if its product design or research information is stolen by a competitor. For example, a pharmaceutical organisation could have spent a lot of money on a new medicine, but a competitor is able to easily steal the final formula and release the product in the market. This could create a financial disaster for the original organisation.

To try and prevent industrial espionage in an organisation, it is advisable to:

- Run proper background checks on members of staff, especially newly hired staff. Conduct periodic security inspections of essential processes. For example, the research and development department must ensure that they secure all their research work properly, and don't leave important papers and information lying around.

- Conduct random security checks on members of staff working in sensitive organisations.

- Wherever possible, reduce the number of laptops used, because they can easily get lost or stolen with sensitive information still inside them.

- Ensure all data is stored on proper file servers and log all activities, such as copying of files to local drives, external drives, removable storage devices and other computers. Advanced logging and alerting tools are available to check illegal copying of files. For example, certain software tools don't allow files to be copied from their source location (maybe a file server) to any other location (for example, a C drive, e-mail attachments) without a series of passwords, justifications and approvals.

- Do not allow consultants, contractors and other third parties to access sensitive data.

- Shred all paper documents before discarding them.

- Use encryption tools to encrypt sensitive data.

- Don't allow removable storage devices to be used regularly by members of staff.

- Ensure that sensitive information is not discussed in open areas.

- Have hidden 24/7 video surveillance in restricted areas. (In some countries, there may be regulations that restrict this).

- When a member of staff leaves, ensure that all login IDs, passwords and access controls of that staff member are disabled or deleted, so that they can't be passed on to other people.

- Ensure contracts of employment have stringent restrictions on use of confidential information and data, if a member of staff leaves. Have a proper information security policy and keep monitoring the gaps and loopholes.

- Prevent smartphones inside sensitive areas. Nowadays, mobile phone cameras are easily available and anyone could photograph sensitive information and send it out as an e-mail via the mobile phone without going through the organisation's computer network.

How can an organisation prevent a disaster relating to paper documents?

On a par with computer data, paper documents are the most important pieces of information that an organisation has, and needs to protect. Paperless offices are still a long way off. Many organisations may still depend on paper for transactions, approvals, signature verifications and forms, so it's virtually impossible to do away with paper. Organisations may have to store paper records for a certain amount of time because of regulatory requirements. Even if the entire technical infrastructure is working fine, if it loses all of its paper records it's still a major, non-recoverable, catastrophic disaster. Precautions must be taken to ensure that all necessary paperwork isn't destroyed by fire, water or other risks. Such precautions include:

- Install an electronic document management system and scan every important document, storing them as a retrievable electronic file.

- Keep all paper records in strong fireproof and waterproof storage.

- Wherever possible, reduce and simplify the number of paper forms and documents.

- Have a quarterly or half yearly paper clean up exercise throughout the organisation to eliminate excess paper, but first ensuring that everyone knows what they can't throw away.

- Do not store any paper records near electrical systems, or hot and humid areas.

- In countries affected, ensure bugs, mice, termites and cockroaches do not destroy paper records.

- If necessary, laminate key documents so that they're not damaged by moisture and water.

What other precautions can an organisation take?

This chapter has introduced some of the more common types of non-IT disasters that might befall an organisation, but there are countless others, many of which will be very specific to the particular organisation, the sector in which it operates and its geographical location.

To adopt Donald Rumsfeld's simile, there are 'known knowns', which could affect any organisation, but its regular systems and procedures should be able to deal with them. 'Known unknowns', are possibilities which it has to be prepared for, or events that might happen, but whether they are disastrous for an organisation, or not, may depend on its response to them. 'Unknown unknowns' are events which couldn't possibly have been anticipated. By definition, there's little that can be done about the last category, other than respond appropriately when it happens, but there *is* more that can be done about the intermediate category - the 'known unknowns'. One of the best methods is by incorporating rigorous PEST analysis into its annual planning exercise. PEST is a way of looking at the political, economic, social and technological factors that might affect an organisation in one way or another, as explained below:

- **Political** factors might include a potential change of government. For example, if an organisation is heavily dependent on government contracts for its business, what happens if the other party gets into power, or if there's a change of law?

- **Economic** analysis can help challenge basic assumptions about the market - both domestic and international.

- **Social** factors might affect the demand for products and services or the ability to provide them. For example, there might be a backlash against advertising certain types of product, such as cigarettes, fur, or fatty snacks for children, which might affect an organisation if it manufactures those products, or supplies another which does. Perhaps an organisation is finding it harder to get the members of staff it needs, because the local workforce isn't sufficiently skilled, or they can't afford to live where it is located.

- **Technological** developments might also affect the demand for products and services, or the ability to provide them. Is a product about to become superseded by a more advanced rival? Is the organisation relying on out-of-date technology?

The unthinkable does happen - organisations do collapse and firms do go bust. In order to avoid that level of disaster it's worth making a point of conducting PEST-type analysis on a regular basis – preferably as part of the annual business planning cycle. This may ensure that the organisation doesn't become so immersed in keeping on top of the minutiae of running the business that it fails to anticipate the key event that destroys its business.

CHAPTER 13: DISASTER RECOVERY AT HOME

'Be grateful for the home you have, knowing that at this moment, all you have is all you need.'

Sarah Ban Breathnach

As personal computers (PCs), internet access and higher bandwidths have become more and more widespread the number of people working from home has increased enormously. Whatever the size of an organisation, it's almost inevitable that it has members of staff working from home. This may be on a regular or occasional basis, such as the CEO burning the midnight oil on the annual business plan, sales people working up their PowerPoint® presentations for a pitch the next morning, or data-input teleworkers. In their own way, all of these people expose the organisation to risks of one sort or another. Any DR or BC plan must also take account of this.

What are the main risks associated with home working?

Working at home brings with it various major and minor risks not usually associated with working in the office. Some of the key risks are:

- Children and pets can cause problems if they can get access to business material. For example, the famous scientist Thomas Edison lost hundreds of his research papers due to a fire accidentally triggered by his pet dog.

- Fire.

- Burglary and theft.

- Electrical short circuits.

- Power outages.

What are some of the ways to prevent disasters occurring in homes?

Precautions need to be taken when working at home, or managing those who do. The following list is not exhaustive, so isn't to be used simply as a checklist, but as a prompt to help analyse the risks and identify the appropriate measures to take:

IT-related precautions

- Do not load games and other things, such as free screensavers on a business computer at home, but have only the essential business applications. Freeware, shareware and games can cause problems and virus attacks.

- Purchase a reliable tape drive or back-up device and back up data regularly. More importantly, learn to restore and verify back-ups.

- Learn how to configure the internet connection and install software and anti-virus programs.

- Have a print out of all important telephone numbers, e-mail IDs, contractor contacts, etc., and keep it updated.

- Have an anti-virus and firewall system to protect computers and keep them updated.

- Have computers, printers and UPS under proper hardware maintenance contracts.

- Download business e-mail to a computer, but also retain a copy on the ISP server.

- If possible, have two e-mail IDs and configure e-mail ID1 to send a one-way copy of all e-mails to e-mail ID2 for back-up purposes. However, don't have a two way setup, because it can crash the mailbox through the ping-pong effect.

- Do not open attachments and other suspicious e-mails that don't appear to be business related.

- Scan important documents and store the images on a CD-ROM or disk.

Safety-related precautions

- Throughout the UK, Europe and in numerous other countries, employers have legal responsibilities in relation to health and safety and other issues affecting any of their members of staff who work from home. In the UK the Health and Safety Executive has published a free, 12-page booklet on the subject; it can be downloaded from: *www.hse.gov.uk*.

- If possible, when working from home use a separate room. Keep all work documents, computers, diskettes, CD-ROMs and telephones in a room that can be locked. For example, a child can easily ruin all business documents for a colouring project or making some paper planes.

- Ensure that the room used for business is fire, water, pest and child-proof. It should also be clean and tidy.

- Do not share a business computer with children, friends or relatives, but have a separate computer for them to use instead.

- Ensure that important documents and other business related materials are out of the reach of children.

- Keep a small fire extinguisher handy.

- Have a UPS with adequate power back-up.

- Ensure that electrical outlets are safe and properly earthed.

- Review insurance policies to check whether the employer's insurance covers losses while working from home, or whether working from home invalidates personal and home insurance.

- Do not leave laptops and other important business material in a car. If the car gets stolen important data will be lost, and a claim may not be able to be made under personal insurance policies.

- Take any other safety precautions necessary depending on the unique nature of the work, home, location and availability of support.

- A home probably wasn't designed to be a work environment, so be careful about overloading the electricity supply with too many plugs and extension leads going into too few sockets. Avoid having leads trailing all over the place that could be tripped over. Try to ensure that the desk, table and workstation meets the basic health and safety advice - ergonomists recommend sitting upright, not too close to the computer screen, with elbows, hips, knees and ankles all at 90° angles.

Document and data management

If working from home on a regular basis, decide how documents and data are to be managed. How are electronic files taken home? Are the updated versions returned to the office in the same way? It's probably best to use a couple of methods. E-mail is fine for short documents, but if doing a five-year business plan it's a pain to have to e-mail large documents which may be too big to attach. Likewise, there's nothing worse than staying up half the night to finish something, e-mailing it to the office and then getting in the next morning to find that the e-mail hasn't worked for some reason. Removable storage devices are an ideal solution to this sort of problem, but they can be a security risk themselves if lost.

Whatever solution is arrived at, thought should be given to how documents that are used both at work and at home are updated and synchronised.

Data back-up for standalone systems

If all master files are in the office, perhaps it doesn't matter to a member of staff if they lose whatever they do at home. However, simple back-up devices and methodologies are available to back up and restore individual computers. Some of the easy, tested and proven practices to ensure data back-ups are as follows:

- **Image back-ups:** A desktop computer can usually be fitted with two physical hard disks - C: and D: For example, hard disk C: could be used for loading all required software and data. This would be the primary business hard disk and the second hard disk could be used as a back-up disk. The entire hard disk C: could then be taken as an image file on to the hard disk D: drive. Special image back-up utilities can be used to transfer a snapshot of an entire hard disk on to another hard disk. If the primary hard disk fails then simply restoring the image can restore the computer back to its original condition. For example, if an image is taken on 1st September at 3 pm, and the primary disk crashes on 5th September, by restoring the image, the computer can be restored to the condition that it was in on 1st September at 3 pm. Depending on the periodicity of the back-up, systems can be restored to the last available image state. The detailed method for this is explained in the sample recommended solution.

- **DVD back-up:** As an additional precaution, the entire image file or essential files can be backed up onto a DVD disk if the size fits.

- **Removable storage devices:** If only a few essential files have to be backed up then low cost removable storage devices, such as USB sticks, can be used. These devices are portable and easy to use, but they will not help to restore an entire computer.

- **Tape drives**: Low cost tape drives are also available that can back up data ranging from 20 to 80 gigabytes.

Sample recommended solution

For large amounts of data back-up it's better to have the following method to ensure complete safety for a system and data files. This will require three hard disks (two internal disks and an external USB stick) on the computer.

How to back-up

- The C: drive should be used for the operating system, necessary applications, back-up software, desktop settings. This disk should not be used to store any important data.

- A folder named IMAGE on the D: drive can be used for taking a complete snapshot back-up of the C: drive through an image back-up tool. This will involve booting with a special bootable USB or CD-ROM and selecting the IMAGE folder of the D: drive as the destination for creating the image.

- A second folder named MYDATA on the D: drive can be used to store all data files.

- The E: drive can be used to copy the IMAGE and MYDATA folders of the D: drive.

How to recover from a crash

In the event of a disk crash the following methods can be used to restore the data:

- If the C: disk crashes, a new C: disk can be plugged in and the last image file can be restored from D: to C using the image tool.

- If the D: disk crashes, a new D: disk can be plugged in and a new image back-up of the C: drive can be backed up to the IMAGE folder on the new D drive. The MYDATA folder from the E: can be re-copied back to the D: drive.

- If the E: disk crashes, a new E: disk can be plugged in and the IMAGE and MYDATA folders re-copied from the D: drive.

As can be seen from the above, this method will have two locations for image files and two locations for data files; hence, there is assurance of complete safety and recoverability for data. If still paranoid there can also be a DVD back-up of data files.

- **Laptops:** The above methods can also be used on laptops, but most laptops don't have multiple hard disks in them. It will have to depend on one or more external USB sticks for taking an image back-up. Some of the recommended methods are as follows:

  - Take a snapshot of the entire C: of the laptop with data folders into an external drive D:. The only issue is the image file will get bigger and bigger as more and more data is loaded to the laptop. Data files can also be stored on a DVD disk.

  - If a laptop disk crashes, simply boot from the bootable USB or CD-ROM and restore the snapshot from the D: external drive.

  - Many cloud contractors provide a web back-up service. This installs a small programme on the laptop or desktop that will automatically back up changes to data across the Internet to an off-site back-up centre. Data can then be restored from this centre if there is a need to do so.

CHAPTER 14: PLENTY OF QUESTIONS

'How can we have wondered about so much for so long, and received so few answers?'

The Judybats

This chapter contains dozens of useful questions that can be used to establish a workable DR and BC setup for an organisation.

Questions on planning and security

(Yes, No or N/A for each)

- Are the existing DR processes adequate?

- Are the offices close to airports or military areas prone to various threats?

- Are the offices close to factories and chemical plants that manufacture hazardous substances?

- Are there proper access control systems to prevent unauthorised persons entering the premises?

- Are members of staff allowing strangers and unauthorised persons into the premises?

- Are there proper security policies and guidelines published?

- Are the offices and workplaces fireproof and waterproof? If not, what precautions need to be taken?

- Is physical security of the offices and workplace adequate?

- Can you be sure that no unauthorised persons are entering the premises after office hours, during office hours, at weekends or holidays?

- Can you be sure that members of staff and other personnel are not passing on sensitive information to unauthorised destinations?

- Is the information security and classification adequate?

- Can you be sure that sensitive information isn't stored in unprotected laptops and local hard disks of member of staff's PCs?

Questions on technology

(Yes, No or N/A for each)

- Are you sure that you are backing up all important data?

- Have you insured and properly labelled all equipment?

- Are you sure that laptops do not contain sensitive information?

- Have you ever tested restoring important data?

- Is there any obsolete outdated equipment or software you are still using which is not supported by vendors?

- Do you have sufficient redundancy on your telephone and other communication links?

- Are you following software-licensing guidelines properly?

- Is access to the data centre secure and to authorised persons only?

- Have you ensured that there is no electrical overload anywhere?

- Are all your critical and sensitive passwords secured?

- Are you sure that no unauthorised persons are accessing your network?

- Is your website safe from hackers?

- Are your employees writing their passwords down?

- Do you have a proper firewall between your internal and external networks?

- Do you have spare and redundant power supplies on critical IT equipment?

- Are you adequately protected against spammers, hackers and other attacks?

- Is your senior management committed to spending enough on disaster recovery?

- Are your networks hacker-proof?

- Do you have proper anti-virus protection?

- Do you have fireproof safes to store backup tapes and important documents?

- Do you have an offsite to store important documents and tapes?

- Is there a proper change management board to approve all technical changes to the infrastructure?

- Are your telephones supplied by at least two or more different service providers?

- Is your office public address system audible in every nook and cranny?

- Are there enough static eliminators in fire hazard areas, data centres, etc.?

- Are your electrical systems and wiring of the proper standard?

- Do you have proper UPS and electric generators to handle long power outages?

Questions on health and safety

(Yes, No or N/A for each)

- Do all critical members of staff know how to operate the fire extinguishers?

- Does everyone know where the fire exits are, and are they marked clearly?

- Is the water supply free from pollution and safe for drinking?

- Are there any harmful or hazardous materials stored in common areas?

- Are there enough emergency lights and torches in the necessary places?

- Is the fire alarm system in working condition?

- Do the premises have 24/7 surveillance in critical areas?

- Is there any water seepage in critical areas?

- Do fire safety experts inspect the building periodically?

- Are there emergency medicines and first aid facilities on the premises?

- Do the premises periodically have a clean-up to eliminate all hazardous and inflammable material around the office and premises?

- Do any members of staff smoke cigarettes inside the premises?

- Are the smoke detectors in working condition?

- Are the paths to the fire exits free from unwanted materials, boxes, etc.?

- Are periodic fire drill and building evacuation exercises carried out?

- Do you have posters, e-mails and newsletters that can be used to create awareness among members of staff?

- Are all emergency numbers readily available?

- Is the cafeteria clean and hygienic?

Questions on financial and legal issues

(Yes, No or N/A for each)

- Do you have sufficient insurance coverage for all critical equipment?

- Can you be assured that all critical equipment is covered under contractor maintenance agreements?

- Do you have sufficient capacity to meet reasonable or sudden high demands?

- Do you have back-up copies, or scanned copies, of every important document?

- Are the important paper documents safe?

- Is all financial information stored in a highly secure location?

- Are professional management practices to avoid staff member harassment, litigation, workplace bullying and legal complications being followed?

- Are you following all government and local tax laws?

- Are adequate budgets available to cover DR and BC?

Questions on people

(Yes, No or N/A for each)

- Do you have a list of all current emergency contact numbers?

- Are there enough members of technical staff to handle major emergencies and disasters?

- Are there any mission critical business or technical functions that are handled or known only by one person? Is there somebody else who can handle those functions if the primary person falls sick, quits or dies?

- Have any members of staff installed personal electrical appliances, such as coffee machines, radios or mobile chargers? These appliances can cause electrical fires by short circuits. Building maintenance staff must be able to educate other members of staff regarding the problems these appliances can cause.

- Do any members of IT staff consume excessive alcohol or take drugs?

- Does it pay the best industry standard salaries to critical members of staff to help staff retention?

- Have you tried contacting all key and critical members of staff after office hours, or on weekends for a mock exercise?

- Is there a crisis management team to handle crisis situations?

- Do- you have a user awareness programme, or training for members of staff on DR and preparedness?

- Is there a specialized and dedicated department to handle DR, BC, CM?

CHAPTER 15: HOW DO I GET STARTED?

'The journey of a thousand miles must begin with a single step.'

Lao Tzu

DR and BC can be complex activities involving cost and effort. In order to get started it is necessary to first have a plan and an initial scope for the activities. A plan need not, and cannot, be accurate or detailed from day one. It evolves and matures over time, depending on experience, what is learned, roadblocks and mistakes. Secondly, most of an organisation's business managers think that BC is primarily the job of the IT department, but it's not. Although it's used extensively in organisations, it's not the responsibility of the IT department alone, nor can they be blamed for business losses if critical IT systems fail as per mentioned. In order for DR and BC to be successful many departments must be involved, many angles explored and budgets prepared.

How does one start a DR or BC programme?

The simple answer is through steps and checklists. For example, the following sample checklist provides a series of high level steps that can be followed by an organisation intending to establish a DR or BC programme. Some of the steps can also be undertaken in parallel. Details on creating individual plans will be provided later.

Step 1: Approvals and paperwork

Before any work can be initiated it's necessary to get the commitment of senior management, cost approvals and paperwork in place.

- Prepare and get approval for a detailed DR or BC proposal for the organisation covering every important or mission critical business function. This will normally be the responsibility of the CTO, CIO and senior business managers. The components of such a proposal were explained earlier in the section on getting senior management commitment in *Chapter 1*.

- Discuss the proposal in detail with the managers of various departments for their inputs and cooperation.

- Clearly agree in writing on what will be provided, and what will not. This is very important to avoid expectation and assumption issues later.

Step 2: Identifying internal manpower

A DR or BC setup can't be established and maintained by one individual, although a single person in small organisations may oversee it. It involves a lot of teamwork and coordination from several areas.

- Identify qualified and trained internal members of staff that will be responsible for various DR or BC activities.

- A DR or BC committee can be formed involving technical and non-technical members of staff headed by a DR and BC manager.

- Clearly identify the roles and responsibilities of each DR and BC team member. Also identify alternative members of staff for each team member, in case any should be unreachable or travelling when the disaster strikes.

• Prepare detailed internal DR documentation for each of the mission critical business functions identified for DR. The documentation must contain what, how, where, when, and why. For example, if the payroll server is a DR or BC item, the documentation must contain complete details for installing, maintaining and synchronizing data into an alternative server housed in the DR or BC site. If there are ten other servers identified for DR, then each server must have its own specific and detailed documentation.

Step 3: Identify external manpower

It's also important and necessary to involve external manpower, such as contractors and consultants, to assist the organisation with its DR and BC activities. For example, if a contractor isn't able to provide critical spares and technical assistance during a disaster, the members of staff may not be able to proceed further.

• Identify appropriate contractors for each of the critical systems and services.

• Establish clear SLAs and commitments with penalties for non-compliance.

Step 4: Identify an alternative site

• Identify a suitable alternative site based on the various factors considered as 'musts' and 'wants'. *Musts* are mandatory, such as electrical power, telephones, communication facilities, computers and 24/7 access.

Wants will be nice-to-have things, but not mandatory, for example air conditioning for common areas and kitchen facilities.

- Spruce up the alternative site with all necessary facilities, for example electrical power, seating arrangements, telephones, UPS, data centre, drinking water, security, storage and parking.

Step 5: Get equipment

- Buy, lease or rent all the necessary IT and non-IT equipment with sufficient capacity and power for DR and BC activities.

Step 6: Install and test equipment

- Have the equipment and software installed by contractors.

- Configure the equipment to meet the organisation's business requirements. For example, if mission critical data is stored in a database at the main site, then the database server at the alternative site must be configured to be identical to that site in all respects to handle data synchronization.

- Label all equipment clearly.

- Test the equipment with dummy data & dry runs.

- Have manuals, documents, checklists and procedures to hand. A detailed checklist for each business function test must be available. For example, the finance department must have a checklist of the things they need to test in the DR site during the practice run, and in the event of a real disaster. This pre-defined checklist is necessary to ensure that the alternative systems provided will perform their business functions.

Step 7: Maintain the DR readiness

Establishing a DR or BC site is not a one-off task. It must be maintained to readiness at all times. Once the site has been established, it is necessary for the identified team to periodically or continuously maintain the site.

- Establish data synchronization, either automatically or manually.

- Keep copies of all necessary software and documentation.

- Keep copies of every important document.

- Conduct dry runs or practice exercises periodically. Close all gaps and deficiencies revealed during dry runs.

- Keep the servers and other equipment updated and maintained with the latest patches, anti-virus, hardware maintenance.

- Upgrade equipment and services as necessary.

- Decommission any unwanted equipment and services, or add new services depending on business needs and growth.

- Keep the BCP and other documents updated regularly, particularly whenever there are additions or modifications to critical services.

Step 8: Get an external opinion and audit

If systems and policies permit, get an external consultant to conduct an independent audit of DR or BC systems. Sometimes the most trivial issues could have been overlooked, which an independent third party may identify. Alternatively, the consultant could offer a better, easier, or more cost effective way of doing things. They could share some of the best practices followed in other reputable organisations.

Step 9: Tell everyone

All of the organisation's members of staff must be periodically educated about DR and BC. They need to know what's been planned in the event of a disaster happening, and what they, that is, the staff will, or will not, be expected to do in such circumstances. User education can be undertaken through slide presentations, video clips, third party educational services, bulletin boards, e-mail and e-learning. The periodicity of the information is important. It can't be carried out just once and then expect that everyone has understood everything in one go. User education and training is a continuous and essential DR and BC process.

How do I create an actual BCP?

The BCP (Business Continuity Plan) is usually a combination of several other types of plan required by an organisation to prepare for these emergencies. It covers contingencies for an organisation's IT systems, business processes, facilities and people. For example, if all key programmers in an important critical project suddenly quit, then the organisation may grind to a halt even though the IT and other systems may be in good condition. A people-related contingency plan, such as having exit agreements or additional programmers, can be prepared to take care of such situations.

It's possible to get, or purchase[2], ready-made detailed templates and procedures for BC, IT contingency and people contingency. Many of the detailed templates and procedures assume or recommend that every organisation can afford to have fully-fledged dedicated teams for situation management, incident management, crisis management, response, damage assessment and recovery. Such diverse departments may be possible or necessary in larger organisations, but it's rarely possible in smaller organisations to have dedicated manpower for such functions. Often it becomes the responsibility of a single person or a small team to take on added responsibilities for DC, BC, etc. For smaller organisations, simplicity and practicality become essential, and hence it is always recommended to have simple, jargon-free, practical plans and checklists.

Common types of plans

- **BCP:** This plan will usually provide procedures for sustaining an organisation's essential business functions, people engagement and crisis management, during a lengthy disruption. It can also have extensive dependence on IT related processes, because business processes are heavily dependent on IT systems. How to

---

[2] See *www.itgovernance.co.uk/shop/p-1334-the-complete-iso22301-bcms-toolkit-suite.aspx.*

create a BCP is explained in a separate question shortly.

- **DR or IT contingency plan:** These plans are mainly technology related and provide procedures to handle IT related disasters. For example, how does an IT department recover data from an important server if there is a major hardware or software fault? Depending on the nature and duration of an IT fault it may be necessary for the organisation to invoke BC. For example, a bank's main computer may fail during working hours and not be expected to be rectified for several hours - this will be a case of DR. Simultaneously, the bank managers allowing customers to withdraw and deposit cash based on paper forms and signatures is a form of BC.

- **Crisis communication plan:** This plan will mainly cover the procedures and rules for providing information to the media, press and government. Corporate communications is a very sensitive matter and must be managed by responsible and knowledgeable members of staff. For example, if there is a major IT or other disaster in a reputable organisation, regular staff must not be allowed to speak or divulge any views they have to the media. This could have disastrous consequences in various forms. Only responsible, senior staff members should provide information related to the disruption. Furthermore, it should be provided in a proper manner to prevent panic, stock market crash and unnecessary rumours.

- **Security incidents plan:** Organisations can be a target for cyber attacks on their websites or networks, such as a hacker defacing its website. It's necessary to have a proper plan to handle such incidents, such as including a procedure to give a proper press release to the media in the event of an incident.

- **People-related contingency plan:** This plan can cover processes and procedures to handle people-related disasters, such as an accident, death, exit of key members of staff or epidemics. In certain types of organisations, it can even cover aspects such as a kidnap or murder of key members of staff. It depends on the country in which they may be working.

- **Other plans:** This depends on the nature of an organisation.

The primary objectives of any organisation's BCP will be to:

- Ensure the safety of all members of staff and other personnel.

- Have minimum customer or reputation impact, and be in a position to keep essential internal and external business functions alive.

- Ensure that it's able to restore to its business as usual functions as soon as possible.

- Meet audit and regulatory requirements, mandatory or otherwise.

The essence of BC lies in the following thinking:

Our organisation uses 'something' that is essential for our business and revenue. If that 'something' fails suddenly what workable alternatives do we have to continue our business and revenue?

For example, that 'something' can be as basic as a telephone or single computer used by an individual, or as complex as a series of massive mainframes used by a large corporation. Having a workable BC plan is critical for any organisation, because it determines and documents the necessary processes and procedures that will be initiated if normal business is interrupted beyond acceptable timeframes. The interruption could be due to a technology failure, natural disaster, fire or civil disturbance. However, BC need not always be a technical solution, and can even be a simple manual solution if possible or acceptable.

A BC plan starts and revolves around the following thinking:

- What are the things and systems that are considered critical for running our business?

- What are the various ways in which these critical systems and functions can stop?

- What is to be done should such a situation arise?

- How long can an organisation tolerate the disruption? What is within its control, and what is out of its control?

- Who will be responsible for ensuring that such a situation doesn't arise, or if it does arise, how is it tackled with a minimum of financial and other losses?

- If such a situation does occur what are the alternatives available to continue with business as usual?

The thinking and documentation can become more granular by asking more questions about each one of the critical systems to frame a BC plan with individual contingency plans. A BC plan gives an overall picture for an organisation, whereas a contingency plan gives specific recovery details for each of the critical systems mentioned in the BC plan.

In larger organisations it is the responsibility of each head of department, or business, to ensure they have a detailed BC plan for their respective unit. In smaller organisations BC can be on a smaller scale and handled by a limited number of designated members of staff.

It should be noted that each plan is unique to every organisation and can't be generalised into a *'one size fits all'* approach. Firstly, it depends on the nature of its business, and secondly, it's always preferable to have one single document as its BC plan, because multiple documents can cause maintenance problems. It is possible in smaller organisations to have a single BCP document, though the inputs may come from many departments. In larger organisations it may not be possible to have a single document outlining every business function. In such cases it is better to split the organisation into logical functions and delegate the BC responsibilities to individual groups to manage.

A sample BC plan with contingency plans for each mission critical system for a small hypothetical organisation is as follows:

Sample BC plan for a hypothetical organisation

Document date: 15 January 2014

Introduction and purpose: Organisations are subject to numerous IT and non-IT threats and disruptions. These can range from a small to severe scale that affects all business units and mission critical functions. Effective planning and preparation are required to ensure that the organisation is shielded from such events. While it's not possible to safeguard from all types of disasters, it's within the organisation's control and financial ability to minimise most of the major risks that may threaten its mission critical systems that are essential for running its business and processes.

This document is intended to assist in ensuring and initiating BC in the event of a major disruption to normal operations in the organisation. The plan outlines the roles and responsibilities of the managers and teams who will be involved to perform necessary tasks to deal with business interruptions beyond acceptable timeframes.

Document owner: Mr Charles, BC Manager. Tel: 123456; Mob: 07987621234.

Location of this document: The latest version will be available in the following places:

- Main site: Two hard copies in the fireproof safe number 1 situated in the security room, ground floor. Keys available from security personnel.

- DR-BC site: Two hard copies in the fireproof safe number 1 situated in the security room at the DR site. Keys available from security personnel.

- One soft and one hard copy with each of the business heads.

- Online copy on the organisation intranet.

Periodicity of update: Document to be updated quarterly in the last week of the quarter end.

List of all mission critical assets and systems: The following is a list of the entire mission critical IT and non-IT assets and systems essential to our organisation's business:

- All data on servers A, B, C and D, situated in the data centre.

- Communication systems E and F.

- Finance, sales and technical documentation and paperwork (electronic and hard copies).

- All legal documents.

- Key members of staff of departments A and B and senior management.

- Any other important equipment.

Each of the above should have an individual, detailed contingency plan, which may be added as an appendix to the BC plan. The contingency plan will have to be prepared by experienced members of staff who are knowledgeable about that particular system.

Risks and impacts: The organisation will incur the following potential or guaranteed financial and reputational losses should one or more critical systems fail during business hours:

System	Anticipated losses
A	£5,000 per day
B	£7,000 per day
C	Reputational losses and government penalties if not recoverable beyond 48 hours

What classifies as a disaster: The following situations are classified as disasters:

- Loss of the data centre due to fire.

- Major technical faults in mission critical computer systems.

- Denial of access to main building. Inaccessibility of the main site for any reason.

- Loss of any documents.

- Loss of key personnel due to accidents, death or competition.

Constraints: The list of constraints and other factors that need to be considered, for example, staff shortage, travel delays.

Limitations: List all possible limitations of the DR site, costs, logistics issues, for example, limited number of telephone lines.

Risks: A list of risks to be considered, for example, a virus attack in the main site could also affect the DR site.

Location of the DR or BC site: Address, telephone numbers and directions.

What is available in the DR site: List all available equipment and facilities.

What is not available: List all available equipment and facilities.

Who can initiate a DR or BC: The following persons will be collectively responsible for initiating or declaring a DR or BC situation:

- Managing director
- CTO and CIO
- Administration manager.

Only authorised and responsible persons should have this authority.

Scope of this document: This document covers DR and BC planning for the following business functions and areas:

- Data centre disasters at main site.

- Finance applications on the following systems (list).

- Sales processing system.

- Document losses in main site.

- Exit of key members of staff.

Out of scope: This document does not cover the following scenarios:

- Loss of both main and DR-BC site for any reason.

- Earthquakes, terrorism, sabotage, civil disturbances, acts of war and other situations beyond the organisation's control.

Acceptable outages: The following table outlines the acceptable outages for each business critical system:

Sl No	Critical system	Function	Owner	Agreed RPO	Agreed RTO
1	A	X	HR		
2	B	Y	Finance		
3	C	Z	Sales		
4	D	T	CTO		

15: How do I get Started?

For example, a key sales processing system may have an acceptable outage of six hours, so a power breakdown expected to be restored back in a couple of hours is not classified as a disaster.

Assumptions: The following assumptions have been made when developing this plan:

- All stakeholders have already agreed to the minimum acceptable level of service, RTO and RPO for each of the critical business functions.

- All necessary data and documents are held at the DR-BC site.

- The DR-BC site is always in a state of readiness.

- Periodic rehearsals have been conducted and gaps closed.

- The organisation's managers and heads of business have personally verified and agreed that the rehearsals conducted are acceptable for their respective business functions.

- Contractors are able to fulfil commitments during a disaster as per their service level agreements.

- Senior management will provide necessary financial assistance during a disaster or crisis.

Who does what and how: In a disaster scenario, who will do what, what sort of approvals (verbal or written) are necessary, etc.

Emergency team and key personnel: The following members of staff and departments will be responsible for handling and managing identified disasters in our organisation:

- Senior management team: the senior management team consisting of the CEO and the following persons: Mr X, Mrs Y and Mr Z.

- Crisis management team, consisting of two senior managers.

- IT team: the IT department headed by the CTO.

- Finance team: the finance department headed by the CFO.

- Office administration team: the office administration department headed by the administration manager.

- Identified business unit representatives.

- External contractors and suppliers.

Meetings: The emergency team and key personnel will meet quarterly to discuss, approve and finalise all matters, upgrades and new issues related to BC. The BC manager will be primarily responsible for ensuring that all areas are covered and will chair the meetings.

Responsibilities: The responsibilities of each of the above teams are as follows:

Senior management	Responsible for evaluating the seriousness of the disaster or crisis. Declare or invoke the BC plan. Provide necessary financial support. Determine recovery priorities and resource assignment. Communication to customers, stakeholders, board of directors, media, etc.
Crisis management team	Crisis communication: responsible for ensuring that the situation is under control from unnecessary panic. Provide press releases, communicating with the media, etc. Post-recovery communications.
IT team	Provide technical assistance for restoring data. Establish agreed communication facilities. Provide alternative or agreed technical workarounds wherever possible. Provide technical support and guidance.
Administration team	Provide necessary assistance related to material and movement of members of staff, transportation, security arrangements, etc. Logistical support.

Finance team	Provide necessary and emergency financial support for activities related to the BC plan, such as emergency purchases, hiring of equipment, travel costs, etc.
Business unit reps	Responsible for having trained members of staff and necessary documentation to conduct essential operations. Run respective operations from alternative site.
External contractors	Provide necessary technical assistance including spares, on-site support, telephonic support, etc., as agreed upon in their respective SLAs.

BC management team and structure: An updated list, contact numbers and organisational structure of all members of staff responsible for DR and BC plan activities. Also list the alternative back-up members for each person.

Organisation contacts: Contact list to be reviewed for update quarterly, and immediately on any known changes.

Primary	Contact details	Alternative	Contact details
Mr A	Address 1 and telephone number	Mr B	Address 2 and telephone number
Mr C	Address 3 and telephone number	Mr D	Address 4 and telephone number

Contractor or supplier contacts: Contact list to be updated every two months or whenever there is any change:

Organisation	Address	Contacts
Sirius Computers		
Dell Computers		
Sun Cabling Corp		

Critical document locations: The following table contains the document locations of all mission critical business functions:

Documents of	Location
Finance department	Fire safe 1
Sales department	Fire safe 2
Technical manuals	Fire safe 3
Passwords	Fire safe 4

DR-BC plan scenarios: The document covers a high level DR-BC plan for the following scenarios (detailed contingency plans for each are available in the appendix of the plan):

Scenario 1: Loss of finance applications	
Probability	Medium
Business owner	Mr A, finance manager
Impact	High
Possible causes	Virus, disk crash, power failure
Functions affected	Payroll, payments
RTO and RPO	One business day

Scenario 1: Loss of finance applications	
Recovery	Expected beyond one day
Action	Start manual and paper-based processes if possible. If not, move finance members of staff to BC site to use alternative systems. Inform all senior managers about what has happened and when it's likely to recover. Call contractor X.
Responsibilities	Finance manager
Mitigation, alternatives	Department to use standby finance system in BC site. Paper entries also to be done for post-recovery operations.
Post-recovery	Differential data to be uploaded to main system

Scenario 2: Loss of key project members of staff	
Probability	Medium
Business owner	Mr X, project head
Impact	High
Possible causes	Competition, accident, resignations
Functions affected	Project A
Time to get equivalent members of staff	One month
Recovery	
Action	Lease other department members of staff part-time.
	HR to hire additional programmers from ABC consultancy immediately.
	Ensure full and proper written handover to person or persons taking over.
	Inform customers about possible delays in shipment and other issues.
Responsibilities	Respective project managers
Mitigation and alternatives	Have additional members of staff to handle such emergencies
Post-recovery	

Scenario 3: Loss of data centre	
Probability	Medium
Business owner	Mr A, finance manager
Impact	High
Possible causes	Fire, major power failure, LAN failure
Functions affected	All
RTO and RPO	One business day
Recovery	Expected beyond one day
Action	Move all mission critical departments to BC site. Inform all senior managers about what has happened and when it's likely to recover. Inform customers about possible delays in shipment and other issues. Call Contractors X, Y and Z.
Responsibilities	CTO
Mitigation and alternatives	All mission critical business functions to work from BC site until data centre is rectified. Paper entries also to be done for post-recovery operations.

Post-recovery	Differential data to be uploaded to main system.

Similar tables with additional information can be prepared for each mission critical business functions for DR-BC. Each of the above scenarios should have a contingency plan with detailed procedures and plans.

Staff member evacuation: Members of staff are expected to evacuate the building if the main siren is switched on.

In the event that it becomes essential to evacuate all members of staff due to a fire, bomb threat or some other emergency it's essential to have a proper evacuation procedure clearly documented and made available to all. Each member of staff must be trained on the evacuation procedure by making them aware of all the fire and emergency exits, assembly points and safety precautions.

Assembly point: The following is the assembly point for members of staff after evacuation until further instructions are provided:

- Football ground near station: address.

A safe assembly point within reasonable walking distance from the organisation's main building should be identified. Each member of staff has been provided with a booklet outlining the evacuation procedure, assembly location and what to do and not what to do. An evacuation rehearsal has to be conducted by the BC Team every quarter.

Crisis communication: to be done by the crisis management team, headed by Mr Thomas.

Coverage: Who needs to be informed about what? Who will inform the customers, the media and other stakeholders? This is to prevent rumours and other inappropriate information leaks that can have serious reputation repercussions and exacerbate the crisis. For example, a journalist can blow a minor issue out of proportion causing serious public relation issues.

Awareness training: Awareness training regarding DR and BC is to be conducted every quarter by the training department.

Dry run schedule: All departments must conduct a mock rehearsal of their respective business functions at the BC site every quarter. The results and issues must be submitted to the BC manager for resolution or work-around.

Reports: Necessary reports and action items after each mock run.

Restoration phase: After the recovery of the main systems it will be necessary to terminate the BC activities and resume normal functions. This will involve the reverse of various activities done during initiation of the BCP. Some of the activities will be as follows:

- Stopping the activities in the DR-BC site.

- Relocation to main site.

- Restoration or re-entry of differential data into the main site systems.

- Informing customers, stakeholders and media.

- Informing all relevant departments and members of staff.

- Unwinding activities.

- Resumption of normal functions at main site.

- Learning exercises.

How is an IT contingency plan prepared?

A BC plan should mainly provide a high level overview to senior management about an organisation's overall BC capability, or lack of it. It shouldn't directly contain detailed technical information that can only be understood by members of IT staff. This requires an IT contingency plan that provides the IT details to recover each critical IT system. This plan is usually very specific and goes into granular details that only department specialists can understand and invoke. However, it will be an important part of a BC plan.

The BC plan can also contain other plans, such as people and non-IT contingency plans. All the contingency plans can become important components of the overall BC plan. For example, if there is a critical finance server running an important application, a proper IT contingency plan is needed to cover emergencies like disk crashes, virus attacks, data corruption or power supply failures for only that specific application. Similarly, a people related contingency plan could have specifics on how to handle people-related issues, such as sudden death, resignations or accidents involving key members of staff.

Sample IT contingency plan for a mission critical server

Purpose: This is a contingency plan for the mission critical finance system running the Star Application that's used by all finance, sales and senior management. Interruption to this system beyond acceptable limits during business hours can result in significant financial and other losses to the organisation. This document is part of the overall BC plan for the organisation.

SYSTEM NAME: FS-1	
A. GENERAL DETAILS	
Asset number	45
Computer name	FS-1
Operating system	Windows Server 2008
Location	Data centre – main rack
Insurance details	ABCD
Hardware support vendor details	Address and telephone
Hardware support contract number	36
Contract validity	Jan 2014 to Dec 2014
Spares available on site	One disk and one power supply inside the spares cabinet

DR machine available?	Available in readiness in DR site
Data backup	Every night at 11 pm on attached tape drive. Image back-up every weekend
Data sync to DR server	Every morning at 2 am automatic. Complete data is synchronized
Software media and manuals	Available in data centre and duplicate in DR site
Critical application	Star application Version 5
Software vendor	Star Systems, address, telephone
System owner	Finance department
Importance	High
Recovery priority	High
Possible failures	Disk crash Data corruption File deletion Power supply failures Entire system loss
Areas affected by this system failure	Sales department Finance department Order processing

Approximate number of users affected	100+
Server maintained by vendor	Star Computers, address, telephone
Maintenance details	9 am to 6 pm Monday to Friday only
Vendor coverage	All hardware
All IT problems to be notified to	Finance department; telephone: 777
Other info 1	
Other info 2	

B. IT CONTINGENCIES	
TYPE	**PLAN**
Disk crash	Re-activate disk if possible.
	If not possible, call contractor support on 2345678 to replace failed disk or other component with disk of 36 gigabytes part number-2345.
	Mention support contract number 36 if asked by contractor.
	Restore data from previous day's tape or last image. Restore complete data from

	session-1 from tape. How to restore: refer to RESTORE-FS1.DOC.
Power failure	Call contractor to replace power supply. Verify whether data is intact. Restore previous day's data if corrupt. How to restore: refer to RESTORE-FS1.DOC.
Major problem: server not recoverable for > 48 hours	Inform BC Manager Members of staff to use alternative server BC-FS1 in DR-BCP site until main system can be rectified or recovered. Differential data to be keyed in manually after main system is restored. Call contractor and inform of situation and to seek assistance. If main server has been totally destroyed inform finance department to initiate insurance claims for Asset Number 45. Continue further operations from BC site or transfer system to main site as appropriate.

Similar plans with more granular details as applicable can be prepared for each of the mission critical IT systems owned by the organisation.

What is a mock run and how is it conducted?

After establishing a DR or BC site it's absolutely necessary to keep it in readiness at all times. It's not a one-off exercise done to suit an audit, or simply to please somebody. Conducting mock runs can give valuable insights and bring out various surprises and highlight serious gaps. It is necessary to conduct periodic mock runs involving all relevant members of staff to prove or disprove that the alternative site is capable of handling a disaster scenario. Some of the important points to be noted are:

- Planned mock runs must be conducted periodically – perhaps quarterly.

- Surprise mock runs can also be conducted to establish any deficiencies.

- Surprises and deficiencies can be observed.

- All gaps and deficiencies noted must be corrected as soon as possible.

- End-users and relevant members of staff will then be aware of what to do in a disaster situation.

- Senior management and stakeholders can be convinced of BC in the event of disasters.

- Contractor commitments can be checked to see if they can actually deliver.

Steps to conduct a mock run

- Plan a convenient date, time and duration.

- Inform all members of the BCM team.

- Inform all relevant members of staff and end-user departments who will be necessary for conducting mock tests on their respective systems. For example, the finance department staff will be required for testing the payroll systems.

- Get attendance commitment from all concerned.

- Arrange transportation and other facilities.

- Technically or logistically disconnect the main systems from the DR site. The assumption is that the main site has been hit with a disaster and all departments have to conduct essential business operations from the alternative site.

- Inform the relevant members of staff to begin their respective tests from the pre-defined checklists they have been provided with, for example payroll checklist and sales checklist.

- Inform the relevant members of staff to note down all issues, major and minor, in a clear document, form or template.

- After the mock run is over analyse the issues and problems experienced by each department or business unit.

- Make a list of top priority issues and problems and arrange to resolve them as soon as possible.

- Conduct another mock run after resolving major issues.

- Get a sign-off on things that meet requirements.

- The cycle and mock runs can go on periodically until the alternative site is a fully tested and proven DR-BC site.

How often should the DR or BC plan be updated?

As DR and BC processes are ongoing exercises, the plan should be reviewed and updated at regular intervals. It should also be immediately updated when there are any changes to the infrastructure or business processes, or when critical applications and systems are introduced or discontinued. Some of the key factors requiring an update of the DR and BC plan can be:

- Addition of a new critical project or department in the organisation. Study the requirements of the new project and make appropriate DRP and BC arrangements.

- Increase or decrease in critical IT equipment.

- Decommissioning of a project. If a project is being shelved for some reason, remove the DRP and BC portions of that project.

- Increase in members of staff, equipment, bandwidth, branch offices, etc.

- Increase or decrease in number of critical software applications.

Basically, any change should prompt an update.

What should a BC/DR checklist consist of?

The main function of checklists for DR or BC should be as a guide to checking, handling and preventing disasters. The following checklists should always be ready to hand and updated:

- List of all key personnel: contact telephone numbers, pagers, home addresses, etc. Update the list periodically and ensure that all members of staff associated with DR and BC keep the list with them at all times.

- List of emergency telephone numbers: hospitals, fire services, police, ambulances, etc.

- List of critical contractors: telephone numbers, contact lists, e-mail addresses, etc.

- List of critical services: Those critical services that the organisation must resume immediately, and those that can wait.

- Contingency plans for each of the critical systems and services.

- Who, what, when, where and how will business resume.

- List of essential documents, IT equipment, etc.

- List of customers, senior management and external agencies to be notified in the event of a major disaster.

... Plus any other lists that may be needed. All these lists have to be verified and updated regularly.

Sample useful checklists

Below are a few useful and simple templates, checklists and tables that can be used to kick-start DR in an organisation. Note that these templates are not exhaustive or highly detailed. However, they are enough to start the data collection, and additional sections can be added as appropriate to a particular organisation.

All these checklists can become components of an overall BC plan.

Important contractors list

It's necessary for organisations to have an up-to-date contractor list with telephone numbers, contact names, e-mails, mobile phone numbers and other contact details.

Contractor	Area	Contact details
Contractor 1	All IBM servers	
Contractor 2	Oracle applications	
Contractor 3	Desktop support	
Contractor 4	Communication support	

Contractor selection checklist

Selecting the right contractor for support is of the utmost importance to any organisation. If the contractor is unable to deliver as expected, an organisation can get into serious business trouble.

- Is the contractor an authorised dealer of the product?

- How far is the contractor office from the organisation?

- Does the contractor have adequate support members of staff who are trained and certified in the products they will support?

- Does the contractor offer 24/7 support if required?

- Does the contractor stock essential spares in their local office, or will they need to wait for sourcing from head office?

- Can the contractor be contacted through e-mail, mobile phone, facsimile and the Internet?

- Will the contractor sign a customised service level agreement and provide status reports?

- Can the contractor provide references?

- Will the contractor sign a non-disclosure agreement?

DR members of staff checklist

It's necessary to have an up-to-date list of all members of staff who have been assigned DR responsibilities, along with their telephone numbers and emergency contact information.

Name	Complete contact details
DR members of staff 1	
DR members of staff 2	
DR members of staff 3	
DR members of staff 4	
DR members of staff 5	

Critical systems checklist

Organisations must be able to identify all their critical systems to decide what is of high priority to the business.

DRP-BCP item	Remarks
List of all mission critical systems that require DR and BC	• Payroll system • Billing system • Sales system
Business priority	Very high
DR-BCP location	Address
Available DR systems in DR-BCP location	• Computer 1: Payroll • Computer 2: Billing • Computer 3: Sales
Data synchronisation between main and DR site	To be done by DR team every night and success or failure recorded, verified and signed.
Test documents for payroll, billing, sales	Available in DR site
DR members of staff	Mr X (phone)

and Telephone numbers	Mr Y (phone)
BCM members of staff and telephone numbers	Mr R (phone) Mr T (phone)
Crisis management members of staff and telephone numbers	Mr G (phone) Mr S (phone)
Important contractors and telephone numbers	Contractor 1 Contractor 2
Accepted RTO and RPO	RTO: One business day RPO: Two business days
DR-BCP document location	Folder DRP on Server 1 CD-ROM in Fireproof safe 1 Printouts in DR location
DR-BCP meeting	Last Wednesday, every month
DR exercise	To be done every quarter by Finance and Sales teams
Other info 1	

Other info 2	

Important data checklist

It's necessary to identify the organisation's important data and how it's protected against disasters.

Data DRP item	Remarks
List of all important data	Complete payroll database Complete billing database Complete sales database All folders on file servers 1 and 2 E-mail folder on e-mail server 1
Method of back-up	Full back-up every day Tape drive and image file method Separate tape for each day
Frequency	Daily overnight complete back-ups
Tape storage	Fireproof safe off-site
Data restore test	A sizeable amount of data to be restored to a test location from every back-up tape every month and results recorded.
Image backups of important servers	Every fortnight after business hours

Standby equipment	Hard disks and power supplies
	Spare server
	Spare tape drive

Restore test template

Simply taking data back-ups regularly is not enough. It's necessary to periodically restore some data and verify the results. The simple table below can be used to conduct a restore test of every back-up tape. The table can be used for every server that's backed up. Data from each server's back-up tape can be restored to a test location and the status recorded.

Sl No	Item	Remarks
1	Server name	FS1
2	Type	Finance server
3	Data selected for restore	D:\Payroll
4	Destination for restoring	E:\TEST on server FSTEST
5	Megabytes	2 GB
6	Restore status	Successful
7	Date	18 March 2014

Communication checklist

Here is a simple checklist or template that can be used to get started and prepared for communication loss. Add or modify sections relevant to the organisation.

Communication DR item	Remarks
Type of communication link at present	Two direct leased lines, each from different service provider One VPN 50 direct telephones 100 intercom lines via a pabx
Redundant lines	Available through manually-operated ISDN dial-up for the direct leased lines. Not available for VPN, but a dial-up internet connection can be used during VPN failures. All direct telephone lines are from two different service providers. Can also use mobile phones in case of direct lines failures.

Software support checklist

The following template can be used to identify and safeguard every critical, or important, application that an organisation uses.

Item	Remarks
Software name	Domino finance application
Application criticality	High
Contractor	Domino Systems
Description	Software is used for storing, updating and reporting all organisation financial information on sales, invoices, payroll, taxes, payments and other associated financial aspects
Software version	Version 7.0
Contractor contact	support@dominosystems.com Telephone: 7778978
Departments using the application	Finance and HR
Business contact	Finance manager
Installed on	Server 1 in data centre
Daily backups	Yes
Software media and manuals	Stored in fireproof safe 1
Is application under contractor support?	Yes. Contract number: 32
Back-up system	Available at DR site

Data synchronization	Every night by DR team
RTO and RPO	X and Y
Other info 1	
Other info 2	

Important documents checklist

Any organisation will have numerous important documents in paper and electronic format that need to be protected and safeguarded. It's necessary to have an accurate list of every important document it needs.

Document	Importance	Location	Owner
Legal	High		
Finance	High		
HR	High		
Technical	Medium		

Non-IT checklist at DR or BC site

It's not enough just to have good IT-related adequacy at the DR or BC site. Other non-IT related detail must also be in place and functional to ensure immediate switch-over in case of emergency. Some of the common non-IT essentials are listed below. Remember that a DR-BC site will have to be a miniature version of the main site.

Item	Remarks
Air conditioning	
Adequate seating	
UPS power	
Diesel generator	
Adequate telephones	
Storage space	
Transport arrangements	
Cafeteria and eating arrangements	
Toilets	
Drinking water	
Building security	
Stationery items	

APPENDIX 1: DISASTER RECOVERY TRAINING AND CERTIFICATION

'I was thrown out of college for cheating on the metaphysics exam; I looked into the soul of the boy sitting next to me.'

Woody Allen

Though an organisation may have sufficient internal skills and expertise to provide in-house DR, it should still have the relevant members of staff trained and certified on DR. Similar to Microsoft®, Novell, Cisco and other training and certification, DR training and certification is becoming popular, and even mandatory in many organisations. Such training provides organisations with international best practices and recommendations, case studies and methods to implement DR and BC. Secondly, it helps prevent an organisation from reinventing the wheel.

When selecting consultants for DR, it's highly recommended to select those with proper DR certifications and relevant experience in the respective fields.

Today there are several organisations worldwide that provide consultancy and training in DR and BC practices. However, there are two international organisations that specialise in all aspects of DR and BC. Outline details of the organisations are provided overleaf. The reader is recommended to visit the respective websites for information on the latest courses, study material and fees for the various courses.

Appendix 1: Disaster Recovery Training and Certification

DRI International (*www.drii.org*)

DRI is a reputable organisation dedicated to providing certification and education in the field of DR and BC. DRI International's certification programmes acknowledge an individual's effort to achieve a professional level of competence in the industry. This recognition, in turn, helps strengthen the credibility of the profession as a whole.

It offers various basic to advanced training courses and certification for professionals. The complete DRI course catalogue in PDF format can be downloaded from the DRI website.

The Business Continuity Institute (*www.thebci.org*)

The Business Continuity Institute provides recognition and professional qualifications for BC practitioners. Represented in several countries, its membership brings various benefits to professionals including recognition, networking, education and knowledge. The site also offers newsletters and best practice guidance.

Other courses and sources

The wealth of information available regarding DR and BC is simply enormous. Organisations and industries are slowly realising the immense importance of having members of staff and departments to look after DR and BC.

In addition to the above organisations, various other institutes, universities, consultancies and commercial training providers offer courses and certifications in DR, BC, emergency planning, etc. Many larger organisations have also developed in-house training and courses on DR and BC tailored to their own specific needs and nature of industry.

The following are some of the organisations providing training, consultancy and study materials on DR and BC. The reader is recommended to visit the respective websites for additional information.

IT Governance (www.itgovernance.co.uk)

IT Governance source, create and deliver products and services to meet the real-world, evolving IT governance needs of today's organisations, directors, managers and practitioners. This includes training and consultancy, where they are one of the leaders in the UK, offering both public and in-house training.

They are very practical and business-oriented, approaching IT governance, regulatory compliance and information security issues from a management perspective. They are committed to engaging leaders of organisations in developing and implementing information, ICT regulatory compliance and information security strategies that enable their businesses to compete effectively in the global information economy.

Sentryx Certification (www.sentryx.com)

Sentryx is a DR/BC consultancy and training firm offering various training courses. It's dedicated to providing a high standard of professional business continuity training and consulting services. Sentryx offers a range of BC training products and services including on- and off-site training, books and computer-based training (CBT) packages. Sentryx's consulting services include business continuity health checks, business impact analysis and business continuity strategy and plan development. The courses are designed to meet the requirements for professional development, certification and corporate business continuity programmes. Their business continuity consulting services include the planning process, implementation, plan development and programme audit.

BCM Academy (www.bcmacademy.nl)

BCM Academy is the leading European information institute for business continuity and crisis management. It offers a full range of education, training and courses in an inspirational environment; without a surfeit of information, but rather a carefully balanced combination of theory and practical execution.

Institute for Business Continuity Training (www.ibct.com)

IBCT provides customised, in-house training and workshops for corporate clients, their business units and business continuity practitioners. Each of the instructors has over 20 years of operational business and IT experience; all are experienced trainers and are professionally-certified business continuity practitioners.

Disaster Survival Planning Network (www.disaster-survival.com)

US-based DSPN helps organisations develop comprehensive enterprise-wide business continuity programmes. They are a network of nationally-certified business continuity and emergency response professionals who work one-to-one with top executives, department managers, safety committees and business continuity project coordinators to plan, implement and test programmes. For clients who already have business continuity programmes, DSPN help audit, test and update their capabilities, thereby identifying gaps in their processes and recommending enhancements consistent with best practices in the industry.

Several other excellent DR and BC programme links and books are available at:

www.rothstein.com/.

APPENDIX 2: BUSINESS CONTINUITY STANDARDS

DR and BC processes - as with any emerging science or area of knowledge are becoming more and more mature. For example, there are almost universal or in-country standards in financial accounting, so that an accountant can move from one organisation to another and still be able to practice accounting. Though organisations can frame and implement their own workable BC practices, they can very soon hit certain limitations and roadblocks. There is a need for universally recognised standards and practices that can be adopted and implemented in any industry. After the international terrorist attacks, financial scandals and hacking cases of the last few years, government agencies and business owners have been pushing for establishing fool-proof BC and risk mitigation methods. A standard for BCM has been mooted for many years. Standards remove the headaches of proprietary and non-portable procedures. BC standards establish a sound basis for understanding, developing and implementing BC within an organisation. Furthermore, adopting industry acceptable practices can give an organisation's business manager's confidence that their business is in safe hands, and can withstand both a real disaster and also the scrutiny of a comprehensive audit.

ISO22301

ISO22301 is the latest management systems Standard for BCM which can be used by organisations of all sizes and types. This Standard was developed by ISO/TC 223, societal security (a committee). This technical committee develops standards for the protection of society from incidents, emergencies and disasters caused by intentional and unintentional human acts, natural hazards and technical failures. The Standard is the result of significant global cooperation and input from both the public and private sectors. ISO22301 may also be used within an organisation to measure itself against good practice, and by auditors wishing to report to management. The requirements specified in ISO 22301:2012 are generic and intended to be applicable to all organisations regardless of type, size and nature of business.

APPENDIX 3: MAKING DR AND BC EXCITING

An organisation can educate members of staff regarding DR and BC practices in a number of ways. DR and BC education need not always be some boring, process-oriented work. It can be made lively and exciting. Organisations can spread the word about DR and BC more effectively, and make more of an impact, by using resources such as the following:

Posters

Organisations can, for very low cost, print colourful and eye-catching posters on DR and BC issues and paste them in all strategic locations, common and security areas. Having a DR or BC related poster is more useful and meaningful than having posters of rock stars, film stars, racing cars or jokes. A powerful statement or tips on a poster can become very useful or handy in times of a personal or corporate crisis.

Videos

DR and BC related video tapes and DVDs prepared by various industry experts could be presented to all members of staff, or to a selection of staff. Such material can also be made available as part of an organisation's library. Such videos are expensive, but they're worth it.

Contests and quizzes

Organisations can have small contests, essay competitions and quizzes via a newsletter or intranet, to make members of staff more aware of DR and BC practices.

Reward programmes

Management can initiate reward programmes for members of staff who report potential problems or issues that could lead to disasters. For example, a member of staff who detects a particular problem that could lead to a fire hazard can be given a reward for the observation and escalation. Management must always be open to listen to bad and costly news first, instead of good and happy news. Easy ways like having suggestion boxes, registers and e-mail IDs for reporting possible disasters can also be implemented.

APPENDIX 4: DISASTER RECOVERY GLOSSARY

Term	Definition
ABCP	Associate Business Continuity Professional. The ABCP level is designed for individuals with less than two years of Continuity Management experience, but who have minimum knowledge in continuity management, and have passed the qualifying exam.
Alert	Notification that a potential disaster situation is imminent exists or has occurred; usually includes a directive for personnel. To stand by for possible activation
Alternate Site	An alternate operating location to be used by business functions when the primary facilities are inaccessible. 1) Another location, computer centre or work area designated for recovery. 2) Location, other than the main facility, that can be used to conduct business functions. 3) A location, other than the normal facility, used to process

data and/or conduct critical business functions in the event of a disaster.

Alternate Work Area Recovery environment complete with necessary infrastructure (desk, telephone, workstation, and associated hardware and equipment, communications, etc.).

Annual Loss Exposure/Expectancy (ALE) A risk management method of calculating loss based on a value and level of frequency.

Application Recovery The component of disaster recovery that deals specifically with the restoration of business system software and data after the processing platform has been restored or replaced.

Assembly Area The designated area at which employees, visitors, and contractors assemble if evacuated from their building/site.

Asset An item of property and/or component of a business activity/process owned by an organisation. There are three types of assets: physical assets (e.g. buildings and equipment); financial assets (e.g. currency, bank deposits and shares) and non-tangible assets (e.g. goodwill, reputation)

Associate Member Associate Member of The Business Continuity Institute. This entry level

(AMBCI)   certification is for those with at least one
                     year's general experience within BCM
                     across all six Business Continuity
                     Competencies. Applicants need to obtain
                     a Pass in the BCI Certificate examination
                     or hold other recognised credentials.

Backlog   a) The amount of work that accumulates
                     when a system or process is unavailable
                     for a long period of time. This work needs
                     to be processed once the system or
                     process is available and may take a
                     considerable amount of time to process.
                     b) A situation whereby a backlog of work
                     requires more time to action than is
                     available through normal working
                     patterns. In extreme circumstances, the
                     backlog may become so marked that the
                     backlog cannot be cleared.

Backup (Data)   A process by which data, electronic or
                     paper-based, is copied in some form so as
                     to be available and used if the original
                     data from which it originated is lost,
                     destroyed or corrupted.

Backup Generator An independent source of power, usually
                     fuelled by diesel or natural gas.

Business Continuity A programme which develops, exercises
                     and maintains plans to enable the
                     organisation to:

                         - respond to a disruption with minimum
                           harm to life and resources;

                         - recover, resume and restore functions
                           within time frames which ensure

continuing viability; and

- provide crisis communications to all stakeholders.

Note: the program and its outputs: are based upon risk evaluation and impact assessment; and require management support, staff training and coordination with external agencies.

Or, Business continuity program

Business Continuity Coordinator	A role within the BCM program that coordinates planning and implementation for overall recovery of an organisation or unit(s).
Business Continuity Institute (BCI)	The BCI is the world's most eminent BCM institute and the name is instantly recognised as standing for good practice and professionalism. Statutory membership of the BCI provides internationally recognised status as the valued certification demonstrates the members' competence to carry out business continuity management (BCM) to a consistent high standard. The wider role of the BCI and the BCI Corporate Partnership is to promote the highest standards of professional competence and commercial ethics in the provision and maintenance of business continuity planning and services. The overall BCI purpose is to promote the art and science of business continuity management worldwide.

Business Continuity Management (BCM)	A holistic management process that identifies potential impacts that threaten an organisation and provides a framework for building resilience with the capability for an effective response that safeguards the interests of its key stakeholders, reputation, brand and value creating activities. The management of recovery or continuity in the event of a disaster. Also the management of the overall program through training, rehearsals and reviews, to ensure the plan stays current and up to date.
Business Continuity Management Process	The Business Continuity Institute's BCM Process provides guidance on good practices that cover the whole BCM Lifecycle and combines 5 key elements: 1) Understanding Your Business 2) BCM Strategies 3) Developing a BCM Response 4) Establishing a BCM Culture 5) Exercising, Maintenance and Audit.
Business Continuity Management Program	An ongoing management and governance process supported by senior management and resourced to ensure that the necessary steps are taken to identify the impact of potential losses, maintain viable recovery strategies and plans, and ensure continuity of products/services through exercising, rehearsal, testing, training, maintenance and assurance.
Business Continuity Management Team	A group of individuals functionally responsible for directing the development and execution of the business continuity

plan, as well as responsible for declaring a disaster and providing direction during the recovery process, both pre-disaster and post-disaster. Similar terms: disaster recovery management team, business recovery management team.

Business Continuity Plan (BCP)

Process of developing and documenting arrangements and procedures that enable an organisation to respond to an event that lasts for an unacceptable period of time and return to performing its critical functions after an interruption.

Business Continuity Plan Administrator

The designated individual responsible for plan documentation, maintenance, and distribution.

Business Continuity Planning

The process which occurs, based on risk evaluation and business impact analysis, to identify procedures, priorities and resources for:

- emergency response operations;

- business continuity strategies for the organisation's functions and supporting infrastructure;

- crisis communications; and

- coordination with external agencies.

Note: The planning process should encompass response through restoration, and result in the creation of one or more of the following types of plan documents: business continuity plans, disaster recovery plans, crisis management plans

Appendix 4: Disaster Recovery Glossary

or pandemic plans

**Business
Continuity
Steering Committee**

A committee of decision makers (e.g. business leaders, technology experts and continuity professionals) tasked with making strategic policy and continuity planning decisions for the organisation, and for providing the resources to accomplish all business continuity programme goals.

Note: steering committees in larger organisations may choose to establish subordinate working groups to direct specific components of the overall programme.

Also: Advisory Council, Governance Council, Steering Committee, etc.

**Business
Continuity Strategy**

An approach by an organisation that will ensure its recovery and continuity in the face of a disaster or other major outage. Plans and methodologies are determined by the organisation's strategy. There may be more than one solution to fulfil an organisation's strategy. Examples: internal or external hot-site, or cold-site, Alternate Work Area reciprocal agreement, Mobile Recovery, Quick Ship /Drop Ship, Consortium-based solutions, etc.

**Business
Continuity Team**

Designated individuals responsible for developing, execution, rehearsals, and maintenance of the business continuity plan, including the processes and procedures. Similar terms: disaster recovery team, business recovery team and recovery team.

Business Impact Analysis

A process designed to prioritise business functions by assessing the potential quantitative (financial) and qualitative (non-financial) impact that might result if an organisation was to experience a business continuity event.

Business Interruption

Any event, whether anticipated (i.e., public service strike) or unanticipated (i.e., blackout) which disrupts the normal course of business operations at an organisation's location. Similar terms: outage, service interruption.

Business Interruption Costs

The impact to the business caused by different types of outages, normally measured by revenue lost.

Business Interruption Insurance

Insurance coverage for disaster related expenses that may be incurred until operations are fully recovered after a disaster. Business interruption insurance generally provides reimbursement for necessary ongoing expenses during this shutdown, plus loss of net profits that would have been earned during the period of interruption, within the limits of the policy.

Business Recovery Coordinator

An individual, or group, designated to coordinate or control designated recovery processes or testing.

Business Recovery

A group responsible for: relocation and

Team	recovery of business unit operations at an alternate site following a business disruption; and subsequent resumption and restoration of those operations at an appropriate site.
Business Recovery Timeline	The approved sequence of activities, required to achieve stable operations following a business interruption. This timeline may range from minutes to weeks, depending upon the recovery requirements and methodology.
Business Unit Recovery	A component of business continuity which deals specifically with the recovery of a key function or department in the event of a disaster.
Call Tree	A document that graphically depicts the calling responsibilities and the calling order used to contact management, employees, customers, vendors and other key contacts in the event of an emergency, disaster, or severe outage situation.
Cascade System	A system whereby one person or organisation calls out/contacts others who in turn initiate further call-outs/contacts as necessary.
CBCP	Certified Business Continuity Professional. The CBCP certification is for individuals with a minimum of two years of Enterprise Continuity Management experience in five of the ten Professional Practice areas, have passed

the qualifying exam and have had their DRII - Certification Application approved.

CFCP

Certified Functional Continuity Professional. The CFCP is designed for individuals with a minimum of two years of Continuity Management experience in three of the ten Professional Practice areas, have passed the qualifying exam and have had their DRII Certification Application approved. This certification provides a certification opportunity for those individuals with Continuity Management experience in specific functional or vertical areas vs. enterprise wide.

Checklist

a) Tool to remind and/or validate that tasks have been completed and resources are available, to report on the status of recovery. b) A list of items (names or tasks etc.) to be checked or consulted.

Checklist Exercise

A method used to exercise a completed disaster recovery plan. This type of exercise is used to determine if the information such as telephone numbers, manuals, equipment, etc. in the plan is accurate and current.

Cold Site

An alternate facility that already has in place the environmental infrastructure required to recover critical business functions or information systems, but does not have any pre-installed computer hardware, telecommunications equipment, communication lines, etc. These must be provisioned at time of disaster.

Command Centre The location, local to the event but outside the immediate affected area, where tactical response, recovery and restoration activities are managed. There could be more than one command centre for each event reporting to a single Emergency Operations Centre.

Command, Control and Coordination A Crisis Management process: Command: means the authority for an organisation or part of an organisation to direct the actions of its own resources (both personnel and equipment). Control means the authority to direct strategic, tactical and operational operations in order to complete an assigned function. This includes the ability to direct the activities of others engaged in the completion of that function, i.e. the crisis as a whole or a function within the crisis management process. The control of an assigned function also carries with it the responsibility for the health and safety of those involved. Coordination means the integration of the expertise of all the agencies/roles involved with the objective of effectively and efficiently bringing the crisis to a successful conclusion.

Communications Recovery The component of Disaster Recovery which deals with the restoration or rerouting of an organisation's

	telecommunication network, or its components, in the event of loss.
Consortium Agreement	An agreement made by a group of organisations to share processing facilities and/or office facilities, if one member of the group suffers a disaster.
Contact List	A list of team members and/or key personnel to be contacted including their back-ups. The list will include the necessary contact information (i.e. home telephone, pager, mobile, etc.) and in many cases it is considered confidential.
Contingency Plan	A plan used by an organisation or business unit to respond to a specific systems failure or disruption of operations.
Contingency Planning	Process of developing advanced arrangements and procedures that enable an organisation to respond to an undesired event that negatively impacts the organisation.
Continuity Of Operations Plan (COOP)	A COOP provides guidance on the system restoration for emergencies, disasters, mobilisation and for maintaining a state of readiness to provide the necessary level of information processing support commensurate with the mission requirements/priorities identified by the respective functional proponent. The Federal Government and its supporting agencies traditionally use this term to describe activities otherwise known as

Disaster Recovery, Business Continuity, Business Resumption, or Contingency Planning.

Continuous Availability

A system or application that supports operations which continue with little to no noticeable impact to the user. For instance, with continuous availability, the user will not have to re-log in, or to re-submit a partial or whole transaction.

Continuous Operations

The ability of an organisation to perform its processes without interruption.

Corporate Governance

The system/process by which the directors and officers of an organisation are required to carry out and discharge their legal, moral and regulatory accountabilities and responsibilities.

Corporate Risk

A category of risk management that looks at ensuring an organisation meets its corporate governance responsibilities, takes appropriate actions and identifies and manages emerging risks.

Cost Benefit Analysis

A process (after a BIA and risk assessment) that facilitates the financial assessment of different strategic BCM options and balances the cost of each option against the perceived savings.

Crisis

A critical event, which, if not handled in an appropriate manner, may dramatically impact an organisation's profitability, reputation, or ability to operate. Or, an occurrence and/or perception that threatens the operations, staff, shareholder value, stakeholders, brand, reputation, trust and/or strategic/business goals of an organisation.

Crisis Management The overall coordination of an organisation's response to a crisis, in an effective, timely manner with the goal of avoiding or minimising damage to the organisation's profitability, reputation and ability to operate.

Crisis Management Team A team consisting of key executives, key role players (i.e. media representative, legal counsel, facilities manager, disaster recovery coordinator, etc.) and the appropriate business owners of critical functions who are responsible for recovery operations during a crisis.

Critical Business Functions The critical operational and/or business support functions that could not be interrupted or unavailable for more than a mandated or predetermined timeframe without significantly jeopardising the organisation. An example of a business function is a logical grouping of processes/activities that produce a product and/or service such as Accounting, Staffing, Customer Service, etc.

Critical Data Point The point in time to which data must be restored in order to achieve recovery objectives.

Critical Physical assets whose incapacity or destruction would have a debilitating

Infrastructure impact on the economic or physical security of an organisation, community, nation, etc.

Critical Service A service without which a building would be 'disabled'. Often applied to the utilities (water, gas, electric) it may also include standby power systems, environmental control systems or communication networks.

Damage Assessment The process of assessing damage to computer hardware, vital records, office facilities, etc., and determining what can be salvaged or restored and what must be replaced following a disaster.

Data Back-up Strategies Data back-up strategies will determine the technologies, media and off-site storage of the back-ups necessary to meet an organisation's data recovery and restoration objectives.

Data Back-ups The copying of production files to media that can be stored both on- and/or off-site and can be used to restore corrupted or lost data or to recover entire systems and databases in the event of a disaster.

Data Centre Recovery The component of Disaster Recovery which deals with the restoration of data centre services and computer processing capabilities at an alternate location and the migration back to the production site.

Data Mirroring A process whereby critical data is

replicated to another device.

Data Protection Process of ensuring confidentiality, integrity and availability of data

Data Recovery The restoration of computer files from back-up media to restore programs and production data to the state that existed at the time of the last safe back-up.

Database Replication The partial or full duplication of data from a source database to one or more destination databases.

Declaration A formal announcement by pre-authorised personnel that a disaster or severe outage is predicted or has occurred and that triggers pre-arranged mitigating actions (e.g. a move to an alternate site).

Declaration Fee A fee charged by a Commercial Hot Site Vendor for a customer invoked disaster declaration.

Denial of Access The inability of an organisation to access and/or occupy its normal working environment.

Dependency The reliance or interaction of one activity or process upon another.

Desk Check One method of validating a specific component of a plan. Typically, the owner of the component reviews it for accuracy and completeness and signs off.

Desktop Exercise See: Table Top Exercise.

Disaster A sudden, unplanned, catastrophic event causing unacceptable damage or loss. 1) An event that compromises an organisation's ability to provide critical functions, processes or services for some unacceptable period of time. 2) An event where an organisation's management invokes their recovery plans.

Disaster Recovery The technical aspect of business continuity. The collection of resources and activities to re-establish information technology services (including components such as infrastructure, telecommunications, systems, applications and data) at an alternate site, following a disruption of IT services. Disaster recovery includes subsequent resumption and restoration of those operations at a more permanent site.

Disaster Recovery Plan The management approved document that defines the resources, actions, tasks and data required to manage the technology recovery effort. Usually refers to the technology recovery effort. This is a component of the Business Continuity Management Program.

Disaster Recovery Planning The technical component of business continuity planning.

DRI International DRI International is a non-profit organisation that offers premier educational and certification programmes globally, for those practitioners within the Continuity Management field.

Drop Ship

A strategy for a) Delivering equipment, supplies and materials at the time of a business continuity event or exercise. b) Providing replacement hardware within a specified time period via prearranged contractual arrangements with an equipment supplier at the time of a business continuity event.

Electronic Vaulting

Electronic transmission of data to a server or storage facility.

Emergency

An unexpected or impending situation that may cause injury, loss of life, destruction of property, or cause the interference, loss or disruption of an organisation's normal business operations to such an extent that it poses a threat.

Emergency Control Centre (ECC)

The Command Centre used by the Crisis Management Team during the first phase of an event. An organisation should have both primary and secondary locations for an ECC in case one of them becomes unavailable/inaccessible. It may also serve as a reporting point for deliveries, services, press and all external contacts.

Emergency Coordinator

The person designated to plan, exercise and implement the activities of sheltering in place or the evacuation of occupants of a site with the first responders and emergency services agencies.

Emergency Operations Centre (EOC)

The physical and/or virtual location from which strategic decisions are made and all activities of an event/incident/crisis are directed, coordinated and monitored.

Note: EOC is different from Command Centre (see Command Centre definition).

Emergency Preparedness

The capability that enables an organisation or community to respond to an emergency in a coordinated, timely and effective manner to prevent the loss of life and minimise injury and property damage.

Emergency Procedures

A documented list of activities to commence immediately to prevent the loss of life and minimise injury and property damage.

Emergency Response

The immediate reaction and response to an emergency situation commonly focusing on ensuring life safety and reducing the severity of the incident.

Emergency Response Plan

A documented plan usually addressing the immediate reaction and response to an emergency situation.

Emergency Response Procedures

The initial response to any event and is focused upon protecting human life and the organisation's assets.

Emergency

Qualified and authorised personnel who

Response Team (ERT)	have been trained to provide immediate assistance.
Enterprise Wide Planning	The overarching master plan covering all aspects of business continuity within the entire organisation.
Escalation	The process by which event related information is communicated upwards through an organisation's established chain of command.
Evacuation	The movement of employees, visitors and contractors from a site and/or building to a safe place (assembly area) in a controlled and monitored manner at time of an event.
Event	Any occurrence that may lead to a business continuity incident.
Executive / Management Succession Plan	A predetermined plan for ensuring the continuity of authority, decision-making and communication in the event that key members of executive management unexpectedly become incapacitated.
Exercise	A people focused activity designed to execute business continuity plans and evaluate the individual and/or organisation performance against approved standards or objectives. Exercises can be announced or unannounced, and are performed for the purpose of training and conditioning team members, and validating the business continuity plan. Exercise results identify

plan gaps and limitations and are used to improve and revise the business continuity plans. Types of exercises include: Table Top Exercise, Simulation Exercise, Operational Exercise, Mock Disaster, Desktop Exercise, Full Rehearsal.

Exercise Auditor

An appointed role that is assigned to assess whether the exercise aims/objectives are being met and to measure whether activities are occurring at the right time and involve the correct people to facilitate their achievement. The exercise auditor is not responsible for the mechanics of the exercise. This independent role is crucial in the subsequent debriefing.

Exercise Controller

See Exercise Owner.

Exercise Coordinator

They are responsible for the mechanics of running the exercise. The Coordinator must lead the exercise and keep it focused within the predefined scope and objectives of the exercise as well as on the disaster scenario. The Coordinator must be objective and not influence the outcome. They perform the coordination to make sure appropriate exercise participants have been identified and that exercise scripts have been prepared before, utilised during, and updated after the exercise.

Exercise Observer

An exercise observer has no active role within the exercise but is present for awareness and training purposes. An exercise observer might make recommendations for procedural improvements.

Exercise Owner
An appointed role that has total management oversight and control of the exercise and has the authority to alter the exercise plan. This includes early termination of the exercise for reasons of safety or the aims/objectives of the exercise cannot be met due to an unforeseen or other internal or external influence.

Exercise Plan
A plan designed to periodically evaluate tasks, teams, and procedures that are documented in business continuity plans to ensure the plan's viability. This can include all or part of the BC plan, but should include mission critical components.

Exercise Script
A set of detailed instructions identifying information necessary to implement a predefined business continuity event scenario for evaluation purposes.

Exposure
The potential susceptibility to loss; the vulnerability to a particular risk.

Extra Expense
The extra cost necessary to implement a recovery strategy and/or mitigate a loss. An example is the cost to transfer inventory to an alternate location to protect it from further damage, cost of reconfiguring lines, overtime costs, etc.

Typically reviewed during BIA and is a consideration during insurance evaluation.

Fellow (FBCI)

Fellow Business Continuity Institute. This senior membership grade is currently held by c.125 BCM practitioners. Applications or nominations to this grade are considered from very experienced MBCIs or SBCIs who can provide evidence of a significant contribution to the Institute and the BCM discipline. There is no direct entry into Fellowship.

Floor Warden

Person responsible for ensuring that all employees, visitors and contractors evacuate a floor within a specific site.

Full Rehearsal

An exercise that simulates a Business Continuity event where the organisation or some of its component parts are suspended until the exercise is completed.

Gap Analysis

A detailed examination to identify risks associated with the differences between Business/Operations requirements and the current available recovery capabilities.

Hardening

The process of making something more secure, resistant to attack, or less vulnerable.

Health and Safety

The process by which the well-being of all employees, contractors, visitors and the public is safeguarded. All business continuity plans and planning must be cognizant of H&S statutory and regulatory requirements and legislation.

Health and Safety considerations should be reviewed during the Risk assessment.

High-Availability   Systems or applications requiring a very high level of reliability and availability. High availability systems typically operate 24/7 and usually require built-in redundancy to minimise the risk of downtime due to hardware and/or telecommunication failures.

High-Risk Areas   Areas identified during the risk assessment that are highly susceptible to a disaster situation or might be the cause of a significant disaster.

Hot site   An alternate facility that already has in place the computer, telecommunications and environmental infrastructure required to recover critical business functions or information systems.

Human Continuity   The ability of an organisation to provide support for its associates and their families before, during and after a business continuity event to ensure a viable workforce. This involves pre planning for potential psychological responses, occupational health and employee assistance programmes, and employee communications.

Human Threats   Possible disruptions in operations resulting from human actions as identified during the risk assessment. (i.e. disgruntled employee, terrorism, blackmail, job actions, riots, etc.).

Impact

The effect, acceptable or unacceptable, of an event on an organisation. The types of business impact are usually described as financial and non-financial and are further divided into specific types of impact.

Incident

An event which is not part of a standard operating business which may impact or interrupt services and, in some cases, may lead to disaster.

Incident Command System (ICS)

Combination of facilities, equipment, personnel, procedures and communications operating within a common organisational structure with responsibility for the command, control and coordination of assigned resources to effectively direct and control the response and recovery to an incident. The flexible design of the ICS allows its span of control to expand or contract as the scope of the situation changes.

Incident Management

The process by which an organisation responds to and controls an incident using emergency response procedures or plans.

Incident Manager

Commands the local emergency operations centre (EOC) reporting up to senior management on the recovery progress. Has the authority to invoke the recovery plan.

Incident Response

The response of an organisation to a disaster, or other significant event, that may significantly impact the organisation, its people, or its ability to function productively. An incident response may include evacuation of a facility, initiating a disaster recovery plan, performing damage assessment and any other measures necessary to bring an organisation to a more stable status.

Information Security

The securing, or safeguarding, of all sensitive information, electronic or otherwise, which is owned by an organisation.

Infrastructure

The underlying foundation, basic framework, or interconnecting structural elements that support an organisation.

Integrated Exercise

An exercise conducted on multiple, interrelated components of a business continuity plan, typically under simulated operating conditions. Examples of interrelated components may include interdependent departments or interfaced systems.

Integrated Test

See integrated exercise.

Interim Site

A temporary location used to continue performing business functions after vacating a recovery site and before the original or new home site can be occupied. Moving to an interim site may be necessary if ongoing stay at the recovery site is not feasible for the period of time needed or if the recovery site is located far from the normal business site that was impacted by the disaster. An interim site move is planned and scheduled in advance to minimise disruption of business processes; equal care must be given to transferring critical functions from the interim site back to the normal business site.

Internal Hot site

A fully equipped alternate processing site owned and operated by the organisation.

Journaling

The process of logging changes or updates to a database since the last full back-up. Journals can be used to recover previous versions of a file before updates were made, or to facilitate disaster recovery, if performed remotely, by applying changes to the last safe back-up.

Key Tasks

Priority procedures and actions in a Business Continuity Plan that must be executed within the first few minutes/hours of the plan invocation.

Lead Time

The time it takes for a supplier to make equipment, services, or supplies, available after receiving an order. Business continuity plans should try to minimise lead time by creating service level agreements (SLAs) with suppliers or alternate suppliers in advance of a business continuity event rather than relying on the suppliers' best efforts.

Logistics / Transportation

A team comprised of various members representing departments associated with supply acquisition and material

Team	transportation, responsible for ensuring the most effective acquisition and mobilisation of hardware, supplies and support materials. This team is also responsible for transporting and supporting staff.
Loss	Unrecoverable resources that are redirected or removed as a result of a business continuity event. Such losses may be loss of life, revenue, market share, competitive stature, public image, facilities, or operational capability.
Loss Adjuster	Designated position activated at the time of a business continuity event to assist in managing the financial implications of the event and should be involved as part of the management team where possible.
Loss Reduction	The technique of instituting mechanisms to lessen the exposure to a particular risk. Loss reduction involves planning for, and reacting to, an event to limit its impact. Examples of loss reduction include sprinkler systems, insurance policies and evacuation procedures.
Loss Transaction Recovery	Recovery of data (paper within the work area and/or system entries) destroyed or lost at the time of the disaster or interruption. Paper documents may need to be requested or re-acquired from original sources. Data for system entries may need to be recreated or re-entered

Manual Procedures An alternative method of working following a loss of IT systems. As working practices rely more and more on computerised activities, the ability of an organisation to fall-back to manual alternatives lessens. However, temporary measures and methods of working can help mitigate the impact of a business continuity event and give staff a feeling of doing something.

MBCP Master Business Continuity Professional. The Master level certification is for individuals with a minimum of five years of Enterprise Continuity Management experience in seven of the ten Professional Practices, have passed both the qualifying exam and the Masters case study, and have had their DRII Certification Application approved.

Member (MBCI) Member of the Business Continuity Institute. Those wishing to attain this well respected certification need to demonstrate experience of working as a BCM practitioner for 3+ years across all six Business Continuity Competencies and hold the BCI Certificate credential of CBCI with merit or other recognised credentials.

Mission Critical Activities The critical operational and/or business support activities (either provided internally or outsourced) required by the organisation to achieve its objective(s), i.e. services and/or products.

Appendix 4: Disaster Recovery Glossary

Mission Critical Application	Applications that support business activities or processes that could not be interrupted or unavailable for 24 hours or less without significantly jeopardising the organisation.
Mobile Recovery	A mobilised resource purchased or contracted for the purpose of business recovery. The mobile recovery centre might include: computers, workstations, telephone, electrical power, etc.
Mobile Standby Trailer	A transportable operating environment, often a large trailer, that can be configured to specific recovery needs such as office facilities, call centres, data centres, etc. This can be contracted to be delivered and set up at a suitable site at short notice.
Mobilisation	The activation of the recovery organisation in response to a disaster declaration.
Mock Disaster	One method of exercising teams in which participants are challenged to determine the actions they would take in the event of a specific disaster scenario. Mock disasters usually involve all, or most, of the applicable teams. Under the guidance of exercise coordinators, the teams walk through the actions they would take per their plans, or simulate performance of these actions. Teams may be at a single exercise location, or at multiple locations, with communication between teams

simulating actual 'disaster mode' communications. A mock disaster will typically operate on a compressed timeframe representing many hours, or even days.

N + 1 A fault tolerant strategy that includes multiple systems or components protected by one back-up system or component. (Many-to-one relationship).

Network Outage An interruption of voice, data, or IP network communications.

Off-Site Storage Any place physically located a significant distance away from the primary site, where duplicated and vital records (hard copy or electronic and/or equipment) may be stored for use during recovery.

Operational Exercise See: Exercise.

Operational Risk The risk of loss resulting from inadequate or failed procedures and controls. This includes loss from events related to technology and infrastructure, failure, business interruptions, staff related problems, and from external events such as regulatory changes.

Orderly Shutdown The actions required to rapidly and gracefully suspend a business function and/or system during a disruption.

Outage The interruption of automated processing systems, infrastructure, support services, or essential business operations, which may result, in the organisations inability to provide services for some period of time.

Peer Review

A review of a specific component of a plan by personnel (other than the owner or author) with appropriate technical or business knowledge for accuracy and completeness.

Plan Maintenance

The management process of keeping an organisation's business continuity management plans up-to-date and effective. Maintenance procedures are a part of this process for the review and update of the BC plans on a defined schedule. Maintenance procedures are a part of this process.

Preventative Measures

Controls aimed at deterring or mitigating undesirable events from taking place.

Prioritization

The ordering of critical activities and their dependencies are established during the BIA and Strategic-planning phase. The business continuity plans will be implemented in the order necessary at the time of the event.

Qualitative Assessment

The process for evaluating a business function based on observations and does not involve measures or numbers. Instead, it uses descriptive categories such as customer service, regulatory requirements, etc., to allow for refinement of the quantitative assessment. This is normally done during the BIA phase of planning.

Quantitative Assessment	The process for placing value on a business function for risk purposes. It is a systematic method that evaluates possible financial impact for losing the ability to perform a business function. It uses numeric values to allow for prioritizations. This is normally done during the BIA phase of planning.
Quick Ship	See Drop Ship.
Reciprocal Agreement	Agreement between two organisations (or two internal business groups) with similar equipment/environment that allows each one to recover at the other's location.
Recoverable Loss	Financial losses due to an event that may be reclaimed in the future, e.g. through insurance or litigation. This is normally identified in the Risk Assessment or BIA.
Recovery	Implementing the prioritised actions required to return the processes and support functions to operational stability following an interruption or disaster.
Recovery Management Team	See: Business Continuity Management (BCM) Team.
Recovery Period	The time period between a disaster and a return to normal functions, during which the disaster recovery plan is employed.
Recovery Point	The point in time to which data was restored and/or systems were recovered

Capability (RPC)   (at the designated recovery/alternate location) after an outage or during a disaster recovery exercise.

Recovery Point Objective (RPO)   The point in time to which data is restored and/or systems are recovered after an outage.

Note: RPO is often used as the basis for developing back-up strategies and determining the amount of data that may require recreation after systems have been recovered. RPO for applications can be enumerated in business time (i.e. "8 business hours" after a Sunday disaster restores to close of business Thursday) or elapsed time, but is always measured in terms of time before a disaster. RPO for systems typically must be established at time of disaster as a specific point in time (e.g. end of previous day's processing) or software version/release.

Recovery Services Agreement / Contract   A contract with an external organisation guaranteeing the provision of specified equipment, facilities, or services, usually within a specified time period, in the event of a business interruption. A typical contract will specify a monthly subscription fee, a declaration fee, usage costs, method of performance, amount of test time, termination options, penalties and liabilities, etc.

Appendix 4: Disaster Recovery Glossary

Recovery Site

A designated site for the recovery of business unit, technology, or other operations, which are critical to the enterprise.

Recovery Strategy

See business continuity strategy.

Recovery Teams

A structured group of teams ready to take control of the recovery operations if a disaster should occur.

Recovery Time Capability (RTC)

The demonstrated amount of time in which systems, applications and/or functions have been recovered, during an exercise or actual event, at the designated recovery/alternate location (physical or virtual). As with RTO, RTC includes assessment, execution and verification activities. RTC and RTO are compared during gap analysis.

Recovery Time Objective (RTO)

The period of time within which systems, applications, or functions must be recovered after an outage. RTO includes the time required for: assessment, execution and verification. RTO may be enumerated in business time (e.g. one business day) or elapsed time (e.g. 24 elapsed hours).

Notes: Assessment includes the activities which occur before or after an initiating event, and lead to confirmation of the execution priorities, time line and responsibilities, and a decision regarding when to execute.

Execution includes the activities related

to accomplishing the pre-planned steps required within the phase to deliver a function, system or application in a new location to its owner.

Verification includes steps taken by a function, system or application owner to ensure everything is in readiness to proceed to live operations.

Recovery Timeline The sequence of recovery activities, or critical path, which must be followed to resume an acceptable level of operation following a business interruption. The timeline may range from minutes to weeks, depending upon the recovery requirements and methodology.

Resilience The ability of an organisation to absorb the impact of a business interruption, and continue to provide a minimum acceptable level of service.

Resilient The process and procedures required to maintain or recover critical services such as 'remote access' or 'end-user support' during a business interruption.

Response The reaction to an incident or emergency to assess the damage or impact and to ascertain the level of containment and control activity required. In addition to addressing matters of life safety and evacuation, Response also addresses the policies, procedures and actions to be followed in the event of an emergency.

Resumption	The process of planning for and/or implementing the restarting of defined business processes and operations following a disaster. This process commonly addresses the most critical business functions within BIA specified timeframes.
Restoration	Process of planning for and/or implementing procedures for the repair of hardware, relocation of the primary site and its contents, and returning to normal operations at the permanent operational location.
Risk	Potential for exposure to loss which can be determined by using either qualitative or quantitative measures.
Risk Assessment Analysis	Process of identifying the risks to an /organisation, assessing the critical functions necessary for an organisation to continue business operations, defining the controls in place to reduce organisation exposure and evaluating the cost for such controls. Risk analysis often involves an evaluation of the probabilities of a particular event.
Risk Categories	Risks of similar types are grouped together under key headings, otherwise known as 'risk categories'. These categories include reputation, strategy, financial, investments, operational infrastructure, business, regulatory compliance, Outsourcing, people,

technology and knowledge.

Risk Controls All methods of reducing the frequency and/or severity of losses including exposure avoidance, loss prevention, loss reduction, segregation of exposure units and non-insurance transfer of risk.

Risk Management The culture processes and structures that are put in place to effectively manage potential negative events. As it is not possible or desirable to eliminate all risk, the objective is to reduce risks to an acceptable level

Risk Transfer A common technique used by Risk Managers to address or mitigate potential exposures of the organisation. A series of techniques describing the various means of addressing risk through insurance and similar products.

Roll Call The process of identifying that all employees, visitors and contractors have been safely evacuated and accounted for following an evacuation of a building or site.

Salvage & Restoration The act of conducting a coordinated assessment to determine the appropriate actions to be performed on impacted assets. The assessment can be coordinated with Insurance adjusters, facilities personnel, or other involved parties. Appropriate actions may include: disposal, replacement, reclamation, refurbishment, recovery or receiving compensation for unrecoverable organisational assets.

SBCI

Specialist of Business Continuity Institute. A professional certification granted by the Business Continuity Institute for specialist practitioners with at least two years of full time experience in a business continuity management related profession and who have good general knowledge of some of the BCI Certification Standards.

Scenario

A pre-defined set of Business Continuity events and conditions that describe, for planning purposes, an interruption, disruption or loss related to some aspect(s) of an organisation's business operations to support conducting a BIA, developing a continuity strategy and developing continuity and exercise plans. Note: Scenarios are neither predictions nor forecasts.

Security Review

A periodic review of policies, procedures and operational practices maintained by an organisation to ensure that they are followed and effective.

Self Insurance

The pre-planned assumption of risk in which a decision is made to bear loses that could result from a Business Continuity event rather than purchasing insurance to cover those potential losses.

Service Continuity

The process and procedures required to maintain or recover critical services such as 'remote access' or 'end-user support' during a business interruption.

Service Continuity Planning

A process used to mitigate, develop and document procedures that enable an organisation to recover critical services after a business interruption.

Service Level Agreement (SLA)

A formal agreement between a service provider (whether internal or external) and their client (whether internal or external), which covers the nature, quality, availability, scope and response of the service provider. The SLA should cover day-to-day situations and disaster situations, as the need for the service may vary in a disaster.

Service Level Management (SLM)

The process of defining, agreeing, documenting and managing the levels of any type of services provided by service providers whether internal or external that are required and cost justified.

Simulation Exercise

One method of exercising teams in which participants perform some or all of the actions they would take in the event of plan activation. Simulation exercises, which may involve one or more teams, are performed under conditions that at least partially simulate 'disaster mode'. They may or may not be performed at the designated alternate location, and typically use only a partial recovery configuration.

Single Point of

A unique pathway or source of a service,

Failure (SPOF)	activity and/or process. Typically, there is no alternative and a loss of that element could lead to a failure of a critical function.
Specialist (SBCI)	This membership grade was developed to allow certification to those practitioners who specialise in aspects of BCM or who work in associated disciplines. Two years specialist experience, a Pass in the BCI Certificate examination and a professional qualification from another awarding body will enable the applicant to enter one of the six Specialist Faculties.
Stand Down	Formal notification that the response to a Business Continuity event is no longer required or has been concluded.
Standalone Test	A test conducted on a specific component of a plan in isolation from other components to validate component functionality, typically under simulated operating conditions.
Structured Walkthrough	Types of exercise in which team members physically implement the business continuity plans and verbally review each step to assess its effectiveness, identify enhancements, constraints and deficiencies.
Subscription	See: Recovery Services Agreement/ Contract.

Supply Chain	All suppliers, manufacturing facilities, distribution centres, warehouses, customers, raw materials, work-in-process inventory, finished goods, and all related information and resources involved in meeting customer and organisational requirements.
System	Set of related technology components that work together to support a business process or provide a service.
System Recovery	The procedures for rebuilding a computer system and network to the condition where it is ready to accept data and applications, and facilitate network communications.
System Restore	The procedures necessary to return a system to an operable state using all available data including data captured by alternate means during the outage. System restore depends upon having a live, recovered system available.
Table Top Exercise	One method of exercising plans in which participants review and discuss the actions they would take without actually performing the actions. Representatives of a single team, or multiple teams, may participate in the exercise typically under the guidance of exercise facilitators.
Task List	Defined mandatory and discretionary tasks allocated to teams and/or individual roles within a Business Continuity Plan

Technical Recovery Team
A group responsible for: relocation and recovery of technology systems, data, applications and/or supporting infrastructure components at an alternate site following a technology disruption; and subsequent resumption and restoration of those operations at an appropriate site.

Test
A pass/fail evaluation of infrastructure (example-computers, cabling, devices, hardware) and\or physical plant infrastructure (example-building systems, generators, utilities) to demonstrate the anticipated operation of the components and system. Tests are often performed as part of normal operations and maintenance. Tests are often included within exercises. (See Exercise).

Test Plan
See Exercise Plan.

Threat
A combination of the risk, the consequence of that risk, and the likelihood that the negative event will take place.

Trauma Counselling
The provisioning of counselling assistance by trained individuals to employees, customers and others who have suffered mental or physical injury as the result of an event.

Trauma
The process of helping employees deal with trauma in a systematic way

Management	following an event by proving trained counsellors, support systems, and coping strategies with the objective of restoring employees psychological well-being.
Unexpected Loss	The worst-case financial loss or impact that a business could incur due to a particular loss event or risk. The unexpected loss is calculated as the expected loss plus the potential adverse volatility in this value. It can be thought of as the worst financial loss that could occur in a year over the next 20 years.
Uninterruptible Power Supply (UPS)	A back-up electrical power supply that provides continuous power to critical equipment in the event that commercial power is lost. The UPS (usually a bank of batteries) offers short-term protection against power surges and outages. The UPS usually only allows enough time for vital systems to be correctly powered down.
Validation Script	A set of procedures within the Business Continuity Plan to validate the proper function of a system or process before returning it to production operation.
Vital Records	Records essential to the continued functioning or reconstitution of an organisation during and after an emergency and also those records essential to protecting the legal and financial rights of that organisation and of the individuals directly affected by its

activities.

Warm Site An alternate processing site which is equipped with some hardware, communications interfaces and, electrical and environmental conditioning, which is only capable of providing back-up after additional provisioning, software or customisation is performed.

Work Area Facility A pre-designated space provided with desks, telephones, PCs, etc., ready for occupation by business recovery teams at short notice. May be internally or externally provided.

Work Area Recovery The component of recovery and continuity that deals specifically with the relocation of a key function or department in the event of a disaster, including personnel, essential records, equipment supplies, work space, communication facilities, work station computer processing capability, fax, copy machines, mail services, etc. Office recovery environment complete with necessary office infrastructure (desk, telephone, workstation, hardware, communications).

Work Area Recovery Planning The business continuity planning process of identifying the needs and preparing procedures and personnel for use at the work area facility.

Workaround Procedures Alternative procedures that may be used by a functional unit(s) to enable it to continue to perform its critical functions during temporary unavailability of specific application systems, electronic or hard copy data, voice or data communication systems, specialised equipment, office facilities, personnel, or external services.

ITG RESOURCES

IT Governance Ltd sources, creates and delivers products and services to meet the real-world, evolving IT governance needs of today's organisations, directors, managers and practitioners.

The ITG website (*www.itgovernance.co.uk*) is the international one-stop-shop for corporate and IT governance information, advice, guidance, books, tools, training and consultancy.

www.itgovernance.co.uk/bc_dr.aspx is the information page on our website for disaster recovery and business continuity resources.

Other Websites

Books and tools published by IT Governance Publishing (ITGP) are available from all business booksellers and are also immediately available from the following websites:

www.itgovernance.eu is our euro-denominated website which ships from Benelux and has a growing range of books in European languages other than English.

www.itgovernanceusa.com is a US$-based website that delivers the full range of IT Governance products to North America, and ships from within the continental US.

www.itgovernance.in provides a selected range of ITGP products specifically for customers in the Indian sub-continent.

www.itgovernance.asia delivers the full range of ITGP publications, serving countries across Asia Pacific. Shipping from Hong Kong, US dollars, Singapore dollars, Hong Kong dollars, New Zealand dollars and Thai baht are all accepted through the website.

Toolkits

ITG's unique range of toolkits includes the IT Governance Framework Toolkit, which contains all the tools and guidance that you will need in order to develop and implement an appropriate IT governance framework for your organisation.

For a free paper on how to use the proprietary Calder-Moir IT Governance Framework, and for a free trial version of the toolkit, see *www.itgovernance.co.uk/calder_moir.aspx*.

There is also a wide range of toolkits to simplify implementation of management systems, such as an ISO/IEC 27001 ISMS or an ISO/IEC 22301 BCMS, and these can all be viewed and purchased online at *www.itgovernance.co.uk*.

Training Services

IT Governance offers an extensive portfolio of training courses designed to educate information security, IT governance, risk management and compliance professionals. Our classroom and online training programme will help you develop the skills required to deliver best practice and compliance to your organisation. They will also enhance your career by providing you with industry standard certifications and increased peer recognition. Our range of courses offer a structured learning path from foundation to advanced level in the key topics of information security, IT governance, business continuity and service management.

ISO22301:2012 is the International Standard for business continuity within organisations and defines the best practice for developing and executing a robust business continuity plan. Our ISO22301 Foundation, Lead Implementer and Lead Auditor training courses are designed to provide delegates with a comprehensive introduction and guide to the implementation of an ISO22301 management system.

For further information, please review the following webpages:

ISO22301 Certified BCMS Foundation:
www.itgovernance.co.uk/shop/p-694-iso22301-bcms-foundation-training-course.aspx.

ISO222301 Certified BCMS Lead Implementer:
www.itgovernance.co.uk/shop/p-695-iso22301-bcms-lead-implementer-training-course.aspx.

ISO22301 Certified BCMS Lead Auditor:
www.itgovernance.co.uk/shop/p-1264-iso22301-certified-bcms-lead-auditor-training-course.aspx.

Full details of all IT Governance training courses can be found at *www.itgovernance.co.uk/training.aspx.*

Professional Services and Consultancy

IT Governance consultants have the expertise to help you apply intelligent approaches to disaster recovery and business continuity. We can show you how to operate smartly so that you and your organisation are prepared for the worst scenarios and can recover IT resources quickly and efficiently. We can show you how to put in place processes that satisfy detailed organisational requirements and mission objectives – making resilient thinking part of every employee's responsibility.

To further ensure your total preparedness in the event of a disruptive incident, we can also show you how to create a Business Continuity Management System (BCMS) certified to ISO22301. With a robust BCMS in place, your organisation can continue trading and return to normal operations as quickly and efficiently as possible, protecting your turnover and reputation.

For more information about how IT Governance consultancy can help improve the resilience of your whole organisation, please visit: *www.itgovernance.co.uk/business-resilience.aspx.*

ITG Resources

Publishing Services

IT Governance Publishing (ITGP) is the world's leading IT-GRC publishing imprint that is wholly owned by IT Governance Ltd.

With books and tools covering all IT governance, risk and compliance frameworks, we are the publisher of choice for authors and distributors alike, producing unique and practical publications of the highest quality, in the latest formats available, which readers will find invaluable.

www.itgovernancepublishing.co.uk is the website dedicated to ITGP enabling both current and future authors, distributors, readers and other interested parties, to have easier access to more information. This allows ITGP website visitors to keep up to date with the latest publications and news.

Newsletter

IT governance is one of the hottest topics in business today, not least because it is also the fastest moving.

You can stay up to date with the latest developments across the whole spectrum of IT governance subject matter, including; risk management, information security, ITIL and IT service management, project governance, compliance and so much more, by subscribing to ITG's core publications and topic alert emails.

Simply visit our subscription centre and select your preferences: *www.itgovernance.co.uk/newsletter.aspx*.